AZUSA STREET BOOK SERIES EDITORS
CECIL M. ROBECK JR.
AND
DARRIN RODGERS

The Pentecostal Blessing

Sermons That Prepared Los Angeles for the Azusa Street Revival

JOSEPH SMALE

Gospel Publishing House

02-4227

Originally published as
The Pentecostal Blessing:
or The Holy Ghost as the Gift
Joseph Smale, Los Angeles, 1905

This book is unabridged and unedited from a copy of the original print run.

All Scripture quotations are from the American Standard Version of the Holy Bible (© 1901).

Series Foreword and Introduction © 2017 by Gospel Publishing House, 1445 N. Boonville Ave., Springfield, Missouri 65802. All rights reserved. No part of this book may be reproduced, stored in a retrieval system, or transmitted in any form or by any means—electronic, mechanical, photocopy, recording, or otherwise—without prior written permission of the publisher, except brief quotations used in connection with reviews in magazines or newspapers.

ISBN: 978-1-60731-491-2

20 19 18 17 • 1 2 3 4

Printed in United States of America

CONTENTS

Series Foreword.................................. 5

Introduction: Joseph Smale: A Biographical Sketch....... 7

Author's Preface................................. 29

1. Some Misconceptions of the Gospel 31

2. Modern Conditions 43

3. The Explanation.............................. 57

4. The Pentecostal Blessing 63

5. The Magnificence of Pentecost 73

6. The Secrets of Pentecostal Fullness 93

Biographies of Azusa Street Book Series Editors 113

It is a wonderful life—the life pictured in these pages—and, best of all, the reader is shown how to attain it.

Series Foreword

Cecil M. Robeck Jr.

Over a century has passed since the Azusa Street Revival (1906–1909), the remarkable spiritual outpouring in Los Angeles that became a focal point of the emerging Pentecostal Movement. Pentecostals/Charismatics, sometimes described as "Renewalists" these days, have exploded in growth in recent years, and now include as many as 670 million people worldwide. They are not all identified as Classical Pentecostals, but they have embraced the experience of baptism in the Holy Spirit and manifest the gifts or charisms of the Holy Spirit in very similar ways. With this growth has come renewed interest in the faith and testimonies of early Pentecostals, including those at the Azusa Street Revival.

This volume is part of the Azusa Street Series, which once again brings into print several of the earliest published accounts of the Azusa Street Revival and its fruit. These primary resources, which provide context and tell the story of the revival, were originally published primarily for popular audiences. However, they have since proven to be of importance for those within the academic world who wish to understand this singularly significant revival for the ongoing life of the Church today.

It is my hope that in reading these volumes, you will be challenged in new or refreshing ways by what God has to offer to

The Pentecostal Blessing

you. Sister Aimee Semple McPherson, pastor of Angelus Temple in Los Angeles, and founder of the International Church of the Foursquare Gospel, quoted the writer of Hebrews (13:8) who wrote so profoundly, "Jesus Christ [is] the same, yesterday, today, and forever!" She required that text to be displayed in or on every Foursquare church building. This message—that God is unchanging and that the vibrant spiritual life of the early Church is still available today—was an essential part of the preaching of the apostle Peter when he said that "the promise is unto you, and to your children, and to all that are afar off, even as many as the Lord our God shall call" (Acts 2:39), and which quickly became part of the worldview embraced by early Pentecostals. May the volumes in this series, likewise, continue to remind Pentecostals of their spiritual heritage and identity.

Introduction

Joseph Smale: A Biographical Sketch

Tim Welch

Joseph Smale was the conduit linking the Welsh Revival to Los Angeles in 1905, which helped set the stage for the emergence of the Pentecostal Movement with the Azusa Street Revival in 1906. According to early Pentecostal journalist Frank Bartleman, William Seymour was God's "Joshua" at Azusa Street, leading the people into the "promised land" of Pentecostalism. However, Bartleman identified Joseph Smale as God's "Moses"—leading the people as far as the "Jordan," though he himself never got across.[1]

For over a century scholars of Pentecostal history have recognized Joseph Smale, a British Baptist pastor, as one of many significant figures involved in the chain of events leading up to the Azusa Street Revival. Attention, however, concentrated upon other more prominent characters in the emergence of Pentecostalism, thus overshadowing Smale's unique and catalytic contribution.

Consequently, Joseph Smale's story deserved further research. This chapter is a condensed version of Smale's biography which emerged during my doctoral studies at the University of Birmingham in the United Kingdom, and which is now published by Paternoster in the "Studies in Evangelical History and Thought" series.[2]

The trail to discover more about this Baptist preacher with a Pentecostal ministry produced some enriching cross-Atlantic friendships and collaboration, not least when Darrin Rodgers, director of the Flower Pentecostal Heritage Center, discovered an original copy of this book, *The Pentecostal Blessing*. This collection of Smale's sermons, delivered in the Autumn of 1905, encouraged Christians to seek "The Holy Ghost as the Gift." I had known of the existence of Smale's book from advertisements in contemporary literature. However, after five years of searching, it appeared that no copies had survived.

Thankfully, in 2008 Rodgers contacted me with the exciting breaking news. A friend had found a copy of Smale's revival sermons in a pile of old books in a garage sale in Oklahoma. He thought it might be of historical interest, purchased it for 25 cents, and deposited it at the Flower Pentecostal Heritage Center. Rodgers immediately ascertained the book's significance, contacted me, and made the book available for my exclusive use for the remaining period of my research. Following the publication of my book, I deposited my research files on Smale at the Flower Pentecostal Heritage Center for the benefit of future researchers.

The Pentecostal Blessing proved to be a spiritual and historical treasure trove! The book documents Smale's teaching amid the emerging revival of 1905–1906, containing invaluable historical materials worthy of analysis. Furthermore, *The Pentecostal Blessing* possesses a challenging message which continues to be important for Christians in the twenty-first century.

Joseph Smale: A Biographical Sketch

Smale's Formative Years

Joseph Smale was born into a working class family in Cornwall, England in 1867, the youngest of five children. His father worked as a copper and tin miner; his mother as a charwoman. The necessity for employment forced a family move to the neighbouring County of Somerset during Joseph's early childhood.

The significance of these geographical locations is highlighted, because they provide important contextual background for Smale's formative years, given that both Cornwall and Somerset had experienced "a rhythm of revival," especially amongst Wesleyan Methodists, throughout the nineteenth century.[3] For example, in 1869 a revival had broken out in a town close to Smale's home, which lasted three months with 150 people converted. This work of God was attributed to "the earnest prayers of the Methodists in the town and to the unity with which both Wesleyans and Bible Christians followed the lead of the Holy Spirit."[4]

Indeed, evidence of such a spiritual climate is substantiated by Smale's own conversion in 1881, when at age fourteen he became a Christian "in a Wesleyan chapel, by a Baptist preacher."[5] Soon after that Smale sensed a call to ministry and began to take services, the Lord "sealing with His approval the word preached, by the salvation of many souls."[6] However, by his own admission Smale lacked training in those early years of Christian service, which led him to apply to The Pastor's College in London, founded by English Baptist preacher Charles Haddon Spurgeon.

Spurgeon's College, London

It was for poorer students such as Smale that The Pastor's College (now called Spurgeon's College) had been established in 1856. The lack of money was not regarded as a legitimate reason to preclude anyone from receiving training to fulfill the call of God upon their life, especially if they had an irresistible urge to preach the gospel.[7] After being personally interviewed by C. H. Spurgeon, the twenty-year-old Smale was invited to begin a three-year theological training course in 1887.

Spurgeon's influential teaching on pneumatological themes helped to shape Joseph Smale's own convictions about the need for, and the possibility of, Holy Spirit power and a "personal Pentecost." In Spurgeon's estimation any true revival would unquestionably herald "a season of glorious disorder."[8] Consequently this particular student of Spurgeon imbibed a robust form of Calvinism interlaced with a heightened expectation for God's power to be displayed with an increase of signs and wonders.[9]

The life and ministry of Joseph Smale establishes a link between C. H. Spurgeon and the development of Pentecostalism. The Calvinist Spurgeon could, therefore, be described as an important root of Pentecostalism, in addition to the more frequently credited Wesleyan and Keswick roots. To Smale, Spurgeon's teaching was simply a balance of "Word and Spirit."[10]

On to Prescott, Arizona

Smale was ordained in 1890. His first pastorate at Park Road Baptist Church, Ryde (on the Isle of Wight) lasted only twenty-eight months. In 1892 Joseph Smale joined the growing army of alumni from Spurgeon's College who were going to pastorates overseas.[11] In October 1892, twenty-five-year-old Pastor Smale left England for North America to begin his second pastorate in the frontier town of Prescott, Arizona.

The embryonic congregation, called Lone Star Baptist Church, was spiritually and culturally engaging with the transient population in the busy mining town of Prescott, which was attempting to build an infrastructure with businesses in their infancy. According to the congregation's history, "this made the pastors feel insecure. The salary was low, housing poor and the church members few."[12]

Marriage and Bereavement

Despite these tough pioneering days in the church at Prescott, Smale gained a measure of relief with his marriage to an English bride, Helena Dunham. Helena endeared herself immediately to the people of Prescott, teaching a Sunday school class of young children, leading and speaking at church Bible studies,[13] and supporting Joseph as a "beloved wife, wise counselor, and efficient helper."[14]

However, after just thirteen months in Prescott, Helena Dunham Smale died at the age of twenty-seven, following the birth and death of their first baby.[15] These were dark and painful days for Joseph Smale, having buried his baby and then laying his wife to rest at Prescott Cemetery.

Amidst his joys and sorrows, all indications point to Smale having established a maturing church using his cluster of gifting as a missionary pastor-evangelist-teacher. During his four years in Prescott, Lone Star Baptist Church had grown from forty-three to 125 members, and with his increasing popularity and noted speaking ability, his wider connections brought

Pastor Joseph Smale to the attention of a prestigious church in Los Angeles.

First Baptist Church, Los Angeles

As Smale commenced his third pastorate at First Baptist Church of Los Angeles in 1897, he informed his new church that they were "looking for a revival, and several signs of it are already with us."[16] But despite his early resolve, Smale's early years at First Baptist Church were mixed with extreme contradictions.

Seven hundred new members joined the church in the first five years,[17] yet attempts to steer the prominent church in the direction of an anticipated revival were hampered by a continual stream of church conflicts and personal disappointments. Furthermore, all of these battles were aired publicly in the Los Angeles press, with sensationalized headlines such as "Warfare Breaks Out in First Baptist Church!"[18] These problems contributed to the deterioration of Smale's health and, by 1904, he was at the point of burnout.

Marriage, Separation, and Divisions

Behind the scenes, Smale's second marriage to Alverda Keyser in June 1898 broke down from the outset. They remained separated until their divorce in 1910. Divisions in the church became increasingly apparent, as many factions emerged within the large congregation over various issues, particularly regarding Smale's dominant leadership style. By 1903, the number of disaffected members had grown, antagonistic business meetings were frequently adjourned after midnight, over one hundred members had left to join Temple Baptist Church, and conflict with the area Baptist Convention ensued.

Joseph Smale: A Biographical Sketch

It was during this time of brokenness and conflict that revival broke out. Smale journeyed to the Welsh Revival in 1905 and became instrumental in the revival fire spreading from Wales to California.

Pentecostal histories generally identify Smale's journey to Wales as some form of "scouting" mission. But in reality, his decision to visit Wales came about because of one simple fact—Joseph Smale was a devastated man. Within a decade his first wife had died; his second marriage had split apart; his church was divided; and his health had deteriorated. Smale was a broken man, looking for spiritual solutions to his problems. Significantly, Smale's brokenness helped to set the stage for the Azusa Street Revival.

By 1904, Smale's absence from the pulpit due to ill health was becoming more frequent. In July 1904, the church members agreed to send Smale abroad on an extended vacation for "six months or such time as he shall be fully recovered . . . providing for him a trip to England and the Holy Land."[19] Some members later admitted their hope that he might not return to Los Angeles![20]

Fifteen Weeks of Revival at First Baptist, 1905

After nine months away, Smale was given a grand welcome-home reception by five hundred church members, who presented him with $150 in gold. Then, on Sunday, May 28, 1905, he preached his first sermon since his return. His sermon title was "The Great Welsh Revival," recounting details of the revival scenes he had witnessed a few weeks earlier.

Congregational minutes recorded: "At the close of the sermon, the Pastor invited all those who were not right or felt they wanted to get nearer to God, to come forward and

The Pentecostal Blessing

kneel. At least two hundred people came. Prayer was offered and there followed a general confession of sin and an asking of forgiveness from each other. The Spirit was strongly manifest."[21]

Prayer and praise services were then held every afternoon and evening during the week. Significantly, these services attracted people from churches across Los Angeles. The Holy Spirit's power was evident at every meeting, and phenomena common in other revivals started occurring. The services were marked by frequent testimony, prayer, and praise, and the pastor often had no chance to preach.

The weekly advertisement in the *Los Angeles Times* was altered in 1905 to incorporate the "Word and Spirit" dimension, reading: "The First Baptist Church of Los Angeles is a fellowship for evangelical preaching, evangelical teaching, pentecostal life and pentecostal service."[22]

By the tenth week, with momentum gathering, the church clarified the purpose of the daily prayer and praise meetings: "The subjects of prayer have been, first for a Pentecost; second, for the infilling with the Holy Ghost of all Christian believers; third, a reversion of the Church of Jesus Christ to Holy Ghost administration; and fourth, the conversion of sinners."[23]

Church members disagreed over how the church would be administered by the Holy Ghost. Smale decided that the church should discontinue the services of the choir leader, claiming that the Holy Spirit was instead leading the meetings.[24] This resulted in the choir threatening strike action and the first formal objection to the daily meetings for prayer. But it was lodged by only one of the deacons, along with the revealing comment by his wife, who asked Smale if "these people [Christians from other churches] could not be made to remain away from the

Wednesday night meetings so that we can have our own little family and the Pastor to ourselves."[25]

Many histories give the impression that the entire board of deacons at First Baptist Church reacted against Smale, resulting in his forced resignation. In reality only one leader, Deacon Dozier, requested a special meeting of church members "to consider the Pastoral Relations." But this was voted down by the board of deacons, with their unsuccessful request to Deacon Dozier to "stop his opposition and fall in line with the church."[26]

That same afternoon, Sunday, September 10, 1905, Smale decided not to continue as pastor and tendered his resignation. Aware of the support of the other six deacons, Smale wished to avert further bad publicity for the church. He also admitted to being "in need of a rest," after the strain of two meetings every day for the previous fifteen weeks.[27]

First New Testament Church, Los Angeles

Smale immediately set out to start a new congregation organized along revival lines. Within eight days of Smale's resignation, the inaugural meeting of his First New Testament Church was convened at the Burbank Hall theatre.[28] This was a pattern not dissimilar to other Pentecostal congregations that, as historian Grant Wacker observes, "particularly liked to take over the devil's warehouses—vacant saloons and dance halls ranked high on the list—to turn them into houses of worship."[29]

Joined by about 225 other Los Angeles-area Christians, mostly from First Baptist, Smale had the opportunity to implement church life and practice in "new wine skins," with the motto: "Under the Headship of Christ." According to Smale, the revival of the previous fifteen weeks transferred effortlessly from First Baptist to Burbank Hall, under the power of the Spirit.[30]

The Pentecostal Blessing

In the autumn of 1905 Smale embarked on a preaching series entitled "The Pentecostal Blessing,"[31] clearly stating to the newly formed First New Testament Church that his theology had been blessed and shaped through "the hard school of life's experience."[32] Smale placed a special emphasis on personal, practical Christian discipleship and on ecclesiology. The intersection point between these two emphases, according to Smale, was found in a deepening Pentecostal experience of "The Holy Ghost," which he referred to as "The Gift," which was "an experience distinct from regeneration" and illustrated in Acts 2:38.[33]

Smale observed that "The Gift" of the Spirit was already evident in tangible ways at the New Testament Church through members' unity, the creation of a "Color Blind" congregation, salvation, personal holiness, and obedience to world evangelization.[34]

In December 1905, Smale recorded that "not a day have we had of our organized life but we have received demonstrations." He cataloged specific things that "God hath wrought" by His Spirit during the period that he preached on "The Pentecostal Blessing." These evidences of the Spirit's work included:

    1. The reign of the Lord over us
    2. A pulpit free to declare the whole truth
    3. A people free to receive the whole truth
    4. A really spiritual church

5. A people who will let the Lord work as He pleases, when He pleases
6. A people serving for the glory of God and not for carnal and sectarian display, or the praise and honor of self, or any other vain motive
7. A scriptural unity
8. Soul winning power
9. A deep knowledge of the prayer life
10. Every meeting achieving the sanctification of believers or the salvation of the lost, and most meetings accomplishing both
11. A passion for a world's evangelization
12. Numbers without the fleshly worldly effort to get and keep them.[35]

Joseph Smale's persuasive advocacy for the Christian Church to return to New Testament priorities of prayer and worship, as eminently contained in the sermons within this book, was actively demonstrated at First New Testament Church in an increasingly intense, expectant spiritual climate. By January 1905, three months before the Azusa Street Revival, one person described "a perpetual revival," attributing spiritual manifestations during meetings to the "quickening" and "fire" of the Holy Ghost. The description of the revival, indeed, seemed to foreshadow the coming Pentecostal revival:

> A congregation last Lord's Day morning so carried away in the Spirit that the Pastor had no opportunity of preaching! The abounding testimonies, the spontaneous singing, the frequent intercessions, and

the altar work supplanted the regular sermon. **This was indeed mightier preaching.**[36]

Smale's primary focus in "The Pentecostal Blessing" sermon series was to encourage believers to have a deeper understanding and experience of the Holy Spirit. However, a secondary focus was Smale's advocacy for returning to what he viewed as "primitive" church organization. He critiqued a reliance upon the "natural and cultivated gifts" of preachers and choirs instead of upon the Holy Spirit. He viewed church socials and clubs as unscriptural attempts to attract new members, encouraging churches to instead focus exclusively on spiritual themes. True to his Baptists roots, Smale also critiqued "denominationalism" and the tendency to create church bureaucracies.[37]

The Gift of Tongues and Azusa Street

The spiritual intensity at Smale's church was heightened after Jennie Moore spoke in tongues during the 1906 Easter Sunday service. Moore later married Azusa Street Revival leader William Seymour. Pentecostalism in Los Angeles was in its infancy. Significantly, the outbreak of tongues speech at Smale's church occurred before Seymour's small congregation relocated to the mission on Azusa Street. The arrival of the gift of tongues and "holy laughter" over subsequent months at Burbank Hall came to be widely reported by local newspapers.[38] Historian Cecil M. Robeck Jr. described how "the place was electrified," causing diverse reactions. Some shouted praises, others who had been to William Seymour's meetings at the Asberry house joined in by speaking in tongues, while others "were so frightened they jumped for the doors."[39] Bartleman's eyewitness account added, "the people gathered in little companies on the sidewalk after the service inquiring what this might mean. It seemed like Pentecostal 'signs.'"[40]

Smale and "The Holy Rollers"

By July 1906, such experiential manifestations of "heaven on earth" at First New Testament Church were increasing in number, intensity and extraordinariness. This was paralleled, if not trumped, by reports of the Azusa Street Revival. Press accounts polarized established churches and leaders, dividing those who felt these were authentic revivals and those who were vehemently opposed to what they considered to be deception and works of the devil.

One should not underestimate the importance of the identification of Smale and First New Testament Church with the emerging Pentecostal revival at Azusa Street and at other burgeoning Pentecostal missions works in those early months. Countering criticism emanating from both the daily newspapers as well as the churches, Joseph Smale provided vital ambassadorial support, lending his credibility to the vulnerable early Pentecostal movement.[41]

Critical depictions of Pentecostal phenomena published in newspapers, along with satirical cartoons,[42] also stirred significant interest in the revival. One *Los Angeles Times* journalist, in an article titled "Rolling on Floor in Smale's Church," described the following scenes:

- "Muttering an unintelligible jargon, men and women rolled on the floor"
- ". . . screeching at the top of their voices at times, and again giving utterance to cries which resembled those of animals in pain."

- "There was a Babel of sound."
- "Men and women embraced each other in the fanatical orgy."
- "One young woman jumped from her seat, screaming 'Praise Him! Praise Him! Praise Him!' and then fell in a writhing fit of hysterical weeping prone on the floor. None of the worshippers went to her rescue. She became unconscious and was left for hours where she had fallen."
- ". . . a pretty young woman scarcely more than 18, who seemed greatly affected by the condition of the girl who had fainted. She was fashionably dressed. Suddenly she arose and began to cackle like a hen. Forth and back she walked in front of the company, wringing her hands and clucking something which no one could interpret."[43]

In response to such publicity, opposition mounted among many of the established pastors and churches who belonged to the Los Angeles Church Federation. Robeck explained how the Federation "raised serious questions" about what they and many regarded as "out-of-control fanaticism."[44]

Responding, Joseph Smale decided to publish an open letter to the Los Angeles Church Federation in the *Los Angeles Express*.[45] In this letter, Smale issued a clarion call that "the churches must cease their unholy rivalries, their living for carnal worldly display, [and] their glorying in denominationalism."[46] In Robeck's estimation, Smale was "the ideal mediator between the Azusa Street Mission and the Los Angeles Church Federation."[47]

It seemed as though members of the Los Angeles Church Federation could agree on little except their opposition to the revival at Azusa Street and First New Testament Church. The *Apostolic Faith*, published by the Azusa Street Mission, noted, "in California, where there had been no unity among churches, they are becoming one against this Pentecostal movement."[48] Smale was a bold advocate for the Pentecostal revival during the summer months of 1906. However, Smale grew weary of what he perceived to be the movement's excesses and eventually withdrew his support.

Why did Smale, who was one of the catalysts of the Azusa Street Revival, grow disillusioned with the emerging Pentecostal Movement? The disillusionment, it seems, was at least partly due to personal hurt and theological differences. Dr. Henry Keyes, one of Smale's most loyal friends and supporters at First Baptist Church and the New Testament Church, vehemently opposed Smale's rejection of a prophetic word brought by Keyes's daughter. Smale had characterized the prophetic word as false and prompted by an evil spirit.

Consequently, by September 1906, the Keyes family and about fifty dissenters had split with Smale, starting the "Come-outers" group, described in the press as "outrivaling the orgies conducted on Azusa Street" with claims of power to raise the dead.[49] Smale was moving in a very different direction.

Alongside these events was an underlying question: "Could Spirit baptism be validated?" Smale was consistent in his teaching, even throughout the momentous days of July 1906, that the gift of tongues was not for every Christian. He based this view upon 1 Corinthians 12:4–11, positing that the certain gifts are given "to one" and then "to another," but never distributed to all.[50]

Smale's view on the gift of tongues diverged from the prevalent Pentecostal teaching that tongues, as the evidence of Spirit-baptism, were available to all. This set him apart from the congregation at Azusa Street. Still, Smale was quick to tell his own church that he

> maintains a cordial attitude toward them [the Azusa Street meetings], and will continue to do so as long as God's Spirit works in them. He has a love for every child of God, but is obliged to differ from some of the doctrinal positions taken by the leaders of the Apostolic Faith Movement.[51]

In addition, there is no evidence that Smale ever received the gift of tongues. Whether the gift of tongues bypassed Smale, or he bypassed the gift, is unknown. Despite many of his church members leaving and heading for the Azusa Street Mission and the Upper Room Mission led by Henry Keyes and Elmer K. Fisher, Joseph Smale continued his ministry of preaching and mission work with a heightened sense of Pentecostal expectation.

Holy Spirit Mission Strategy

For Smale, baptism in the Spirit should lead Christians to regain "soul-winning" power, and so, in keeping with his Spurgeonic roots, Smale encouraged the New Testament Church in local and global missions endeavors. Mrs. Davis, "an old woman" in Smale's congregation, came forward to go as a missionary to Jerusalem in 1905.[52] The most significant missions strategy emanating from the revival fires of First New Testament Church occurred in March 1907, when Smale traveled to China with the sole purpose of establishing a "Gospel Mission." Smale detailed his trip in a tract, "An Apostolic Journey in the

20th Century."⁵³ The "China New Testament Church" which was formed on Smale's "apostolic" visit to Pakhoi in 1907 was still in existence when he returned to China in 1921.

Smale's Final Years, 1911–1926

Smale continued to pastor First New Testament Church for several more years after the Azusa Street Revival. He married again in 1911 and, with his new bride Esther Hargrave, left Los Angeles with the intention of becoming missionaries to Spain. After spending the winter in Spain, their plans altered and Smale was invited to become the pastor of an independent church in South London, very close to Spurgeon's College. In 1913, during his short ministry there, Smale established the Spanish Gospel Mission, which continues to operate to the present day.

The Smales moved again, with Joseph becoming pastor of Unity Chapel Bristol in late 1913. This church, with its earlier connections with George Muller, operated along Plymouth Brethren lines. It was a faith work, meaning the pastor "received no stated salary," and its church leaders settled business only "by the consent of an undivided church."⁵⁴ Smale's pastorate here, as elsewhere, was marked by its brevity.

By 1916 the Smale family had returned to Los Angeles, and Joseph Smale resumed ministry at what was then called Grace Baptist Church (formerly First New Testament Church) until his death in 1926 at age fifty-nine. Near the end of his life, Smale issued a severe indictment of the movement that he had helped to start. He wrote, "Pentecostal denominations have committed a blunder in interpreting the acts of the Apostles as descriptive of the Church of this parenthesis age. . . . So untrue an interpretation is responsible for the orgy of disorder as seen in the Pentecostal movement of our times; and the confusion, division and the schismatic life and spirit so characteristic of present day organised Christianity."[55]

Nevertheless, Joseph Smale remained convinced throughout his ministry that the church and every Christian believer needed a personal Pentecost. Such a baptism of the Spirit, in his view, would "baptize with heavenly spiritual life"[56] so that believers could be "filled for the work of evangelism."[57] He downplayed the gift of tongues, not wanting to restrict the work of the Spirit "to a lingual exercise of the throat."[58]

Smale's contributions to Pentecostal and Baptist history touch on numerous issues that are very relevant for twenty-first century Pentecostal and charismatic Christians. Bartleman's identification of Smale as Pentecostalism's "Moses" figure is an enduring reminder both of Smale's significance in the Movement's infancy, and of the loss of his potential leadership after his departure from the Movement in 1907. A study of his life and preaching enables further reflections regarding the seeming dilemma between "freedom in the Spirit" and the organization of Spirit-led activity. The compelling thrust of Smale's sermons in this book provide a timeless and unequivocal reminder to every Christian and local church that we "must honor the Holy Spirit."[59] As Smale believed until his death, God's gift of the Spirit is the key to experiencing true revival with "the Spirit as 'The Pentecostal Blessing,' necessary to the believer's sanctification, . . . knowledge of the fullness of God, and . . . anointing for service."[60] It seems apt to close this biographical portrait with Smale's own encouragement:

> "Oh, believer, be ever going in for more and *more*, and MORE and MORE."[61]

Joseph Smale: A Biographical Sketch

Endnotes

1 Bartleman, a participant at the Azusa Street Revival (Los Angeles, 1906–1909), went on to become the most prominent early historian of the revival. Frank Bartleman, *How Pentecost Came to Los Angeles: As It Was at the Beginning* (Los Angeles: The Author, 1925), 47.

2 Tim Welch, *Joseph Smale: God's 'Moses' for Pentecostalism* (Paternoster, 2013).

3 David W. Bebbington, "Culture and Piety in the Far West: Revival in Penzance, Newlyn, and Mousehole in 1849," in *Revival and Resurgence in Christian History*, ed. Kate Cooper and Jeremy Gregory (Boydell Press, 2008), 225–250.

4 Lewis H. Court, *The Romance of a Country Circuit: Sketches of Village Methodism* (Henry Hooks, 1921), 32.

5 "Baptist Ordination at Ryde," *Isle of Wight County Press Newspaper*, May 17, 1890, 6.

6 Ibid., 6.

7 J. C. Carlile, *C. H. Spurgeon: An Interpretative Biography* (London: The Religious Tract Society, 1933), 171.

8 C. H. Spurgeon, "The Pentecostal Wind and Fire," *Metropolitan Pulpit*, September 18, 1881, 93.

9 Ibid., 93.

10 Joseph Smale, *Our Church Quarterly* (First Baptist Church, LA, December 1897), 1.

11 Ian M. Randall, *A School of the Prophets* (Spurgeon's College, 2005), 94.

12 First Baptist Church, Prescott, Arizona, *The Ninetieth Anniversary 1880–1970*, 20.

13 *Arizona Weekly Journal Miner*, January 3, 1894, 6.

14 Arizona Baptist Association Minutes 1894–1895, *In Memoriam: Obituary of Helena Dunham Smale*, 13.

15 *Arizona Weekly Journal Miner*, January 30, 1895, 5.

16 Joseph Smale, *Our Church Quarterly* (December 1897), 1.

17 "Five Years of Success," *Los Angeles Herald*, February 6, 1902, 10.

18 "Call for Trial of Pastor Smale," *Los Angeles Times*, September 15, 1902, 14.

19 First Baptist Church of Los Angeles (FBC LA), *Records*, Volume IX (1905), July 31.

20 "Bombs for Baptists," *Los Angeles Times*, September 11, 1905, 11.

21 FBC LA, *Records*, May 28.

The Pentecostal Blessing

22 "Church Services," *Los Angeles Times*, July 29, 1905, I.11.
23 FBC LA, *Records*, August 6.
24 FBC LA, *Records*, August 23.
25 FBC LA, *Records*, September 6.
26 FBC LA, *Records*, September 11.
27 "Baptist Boil Still Biling," *Los Angeles Times*, September 12, 1905, II.10.
28 First New Testament Church Los Angeles (FNTC LA), *Our First Anniversary* (September 1906), 3.
29 Grant Wacker, *Heaven Below* (Harvard University Press, 2001), 112.
30 FNTC LA, *Our First Anniversary*, 3.
31 Joseph Smale, *The Pentecostal Blessing* (Los Angeles: First New Testament Church of Los Angeles, 1905); seven sermons are incorporated in this book.
32 Smale, *The Pentecostal Blessing*, 3.
33 Smale, *The Pentecostal Blessing*, 44.
34 FNTC LA, *Our First Anniversary*, 8.
35 First New Testament Church LA, *Historical Number of the Bulletin* (March, 1906), 6.
36 Ibid. [Bold original]
37 Smale, *The Pentecostal Blessing*, 24–34.
38 "Rolling on Floor in Smale's Church," *Los Angeles Times*, July 14, 1906, II.1; "Holy Roller Mad," *Los Angeles Times*, July 17, 1906, II.14; "Queer 'Gift' Given Many," *Los Angeles Times*, July 23, 1906, 15.
39 Cecil M. Robeck, *The Azusa Street Mission & Revival* (Nelson, 2006), 75.
40 Bartleman, 44.
41 Robeck, 83–86.
42 "Queer 'Gift' Given Many," *Los Angeles Times*, July 23, 1906, 15.
43 "Rolling on Floor in Smale's Church," *Los Angeles Times*, July 14, 1906, II.1.
44 Robeck, 83.
45 "New Testament Leader Writes Open Letter," *Los Angeles Express*, July 23 1906, 6.
46 Ibid., 6.
47 Robeck, 84.
48 *The Apostolic Faith (Azusa Street)*, Volume 1, No. 2 (October 1906), 4.
49 "Claim Power to Raise Dead," *Los Angeles Times*, September 24, 1906, I17.

50 Joseph Smale, *First New Testament Church First Anniversary Brochure*, September 1906.
51 FNTC, *Bulletin for July 8–July 15*, 1906, 3.
52 "Indian is a Hustler," *Los Angeles Times*, December 9, 1905, 17.
53 Joseph Smale, An Apostolic Journey in the 20th Century (First New Testament Church, 1908).
54 "Unity Chapel, St. Philip's Bristol," *Evangelical Quarterly*, 229.
55 Joseph Smale, *Truth: Earthly and Heavenly*, (n.p.: Smale, 1925?), 36.
56 Joseph Smale, A Message to Spirit-Filled Believers, In: *Truth: Earthly and Heavenly*, (n.p.: Smale, 1926?), 91.
57 Ibid., 89.
58 Ibid., 90.
59 Smale, *The Pentecostal Blessing*, 42.
60 Ibid., 44.
61 Ibid., 48.

Author's Preface

This little book presents to the reader the substance of seven sermons delivered in the First New Testament Church of Los Angeles in the autumn of 1905. No ordinary occasion produced them. They are not the thought of any one hour, or day, or week, or month. There are some truths we learn but slowly, and then only in the hard school of life's experience. The one here expounded God taught the preacher in what were at first to him some of the enigmatical and perplexing situations of his life. The result has been an untold blessing to him personally and as a Christian minister.

Two questions prevail in the hearts of all true friends of our adorable Lord. How to be at one's best for Him? And, how to have the visible church of Christ as nearly as possible the expression of the mystical body of Christ, which she assumes to represent? The real and only reply to these questions is: "The Holy Ghost." This being so, no truth, more, or even as important, can be considered by Christians today than that of the Holy Ghost. No other study if it be devoutly and prayerfully taken up can yield such blessed results to those who are exercised in mind about their own spiritual condition, and that of the church of Christ.

In the following pages a treatment of this subject of subjects is attempted in the hope of imparting a vision, where it does not exist, of the Holy Ghost *as the one and all-sufficient and divinely ordained Person, and inspiration, to meet the manifold needs of Christian souls individually, and in their corporate character of churches;* and that a faith may be born in such that this blessed Person of the Trinity is only waiting to be rightfully honored by us before he will fill with glory and power these lives of ours and those of the whole church of God throughout the earth.

With this motive we humbly submit these leaves to Christian readers everywhere. May the blessing of the Lord go with them, and their effect be healing and life to all who are longing for spiritual health and power; and an awakening to those who have not understood the truth of the gospel of our salvation.

CHAPTER 1

Some Misconceptions of the Gospel

We confine the discussion to those misconceptions within the evangelical fold, and of such, the ones of major significance, which seriously affect a true embodiment and illustration of Christian life, experience and service. We summarize the subject under four divisions: First, the popular error that all the cardinal characteristics of the gospel for our life in this world are realized at conversion. Where emphasis is laid upon soul-winning work conversion is made chiefly the goal of labour. That which follows consist of such things as church membership and joining societies within the church, and doing some service either in teaching or occupying a place in the official life, and only exceptionally is the convert seeking the salvation of souls. The greatest things to be attended to by a new-born soul are rarely mentioned in the average church. If the ordinary Christian is plied for a definition of the gospel, what is he likely to say? Perhaps he will make note of the incarnation of the Eternal Son of God; the sacrificial work on the Cross; justification by faith; the new birth; the sonship of believers; and with an observation or two upon prayer, the Bible; the church

The Pentecostal Blessing

and heaven, this is the reach in his conception of the gospel. We think we are rather overstating his definition, for with the notorious omissions, of the things of the Word of God in much modern preaching, scarce any evangelical test in many quarters exists for church membership, and the people's connection with the house of God is becoming largely a matter of mere sentiment, and morals, and custom instead of spiritual life. We hope the reader has assured himself of saving truth and knows that the impregnable rock of a "thus saith the Lord" is the only foundation of a truly Christian hope. We are taking this for granted, for our subject matter deals with truth that can only be known after conversion, and is intended to help *believers* on the Lord Jesus Christ. Where the historical doctrines of the faith are preached, and congregations understand the things fundamental to the experience of eternal life, there is not usually taught the splendid truths which in the purpose of God in His gospel immediately follow the penitent's trust in Christ. We cannot be too thankful in our times that any company of people are being blessed from the pulpit with expositions of the saving truth of the imputed righteousness of Christ. But to get even this, sinners for the most part have to seek the mission hall rather than the church. Christ crucified is truth but little found in the sermons of our day. In the few churches comparatively that love the substitutionary work of Christ we greatly wish that a whole gospel were preached. The serious lack, in the ministry of most of the really evangelical churches is that the pulpit has little or nothing to say, about the deep truths of the Christian life. After we are saved, we need keeping and establishing, and manifold inspirations for Christian duty and privilege. But where are the preachers who instruct their hearers on the true method and means. Having had set before us the glories of the work of

Some Misconceptions of the Gospel

Christ *for us*, and having appropriated that work by faith, we need a tremendous work of Christ *within us*, a work unknown in regeneration. What is the gospel? Tell me not it is a life of struggle, frequent defeat, intermittent peace, occasional joy. Tell me not Jesus Christ wrought in strength on the Cross for me, but he can only do so in weakness within me. Tell me not there is no such thing as a permanent unbroken supremacy of the soul over the world, the flesh, and the devil. If your experience, though a child of God, is one of captivity and servitude to evil, there are thousands rejoicing in liberty and having power over all the power of the enemy. Who shall deliver me from the body of this death? Say not we have to endure it and make the best of a bad situation. No, no, deliverance is here and now. "I thank God through Jesus Christ our Lord." *A thorough work in the life of the believer, bringing him now absolutely from under the dominion of sin is possible, and is taught in the Scriptures.* What is the glorious Word? "The God of peace Himself sanctify you wholly and may your spirit and soul and body be preserved entire without blame at the coming of our Lord Jesus Christ." The gospel is not only the grace of justification but the glory of sanctification, not only the blessing of the new birth but the riches of the Spirit-filled life. These double experiences are indeed for us while we are in this evil world. The gospel is not as an old time insurance policy only payable at death, but like—only better—those policies that mature in the policy-holder's lifetime. Let a man take up with the gospel, let him put his faith therein, and he will draw out ultimately the life of heaven, but he may draw out today if he will a supernatural life. In the gospel we have:

> "A religion which supplies
> Solid comfort when man dies."

The Pentecostal Blessing

Also:
> "A religion that will give
> Sweetest pleasures while man lives."

What, then, Christian reader, is the gospel to you. This is the will of God even your sanctification. I bow my knees unto the Father . . . that He would grant you, according to the riches of His glory, to be strengthened with might by His spirit in the inner man; that Christ might dwell in your hearts by faith; that ye, being rooted and grounded in love, may be able to apprehend with all saints, what is the breadth, and length, and depth, and height; and to know the love of Christ, which passeth knowledge, that ye might be filled with all the fullness of God. This can be the Christian's *present experience*. Glory to God.

A second misconception is that the gospel is mainly beliefs for the head and not experiences for the heart. The gospel is *revealed* truth, and such as the "'natural" man cannot receive, yet many a "natural" man thinks he can receive it; and thinks he has received it. When we meet him in reference to it we find his mind mirrors chiefly the truths of religion as nature makes them known. As for his understanding of revealed truths, we find they are so reduced to the terms of finite reason as to be made for all practical purposes null and void. His knowledge of the gospel in reality is only the knowledge of the facts of Christian history. Of the profound truths associated with those facts he is a stranger. His religion is not a matter of the heart. To him consecration, sanctification, separation from the world, a life of piety, world-wide missionary sympathies, and the hallelujah gladness of the saint of God, are not the essentials of religion but the spirit of fanaticism. Yet Scripture says: "The kingdom

Some Misconceptions of the Gospel

of God is righteousness and peace and joy in the Holy Ghost." The "natural" man never rises to either one of these. *One-third part of religion, according to the Bible is emotion.* It is joy, the pure, delightful joy of a renewed heart. *One-third is undisturbed serenity.* It is peace, which is a near neighbor of joy. But of this he knows nothing. The calm in which he may boast is a false peace, for the ground of true peace is the shed blood of Christ. *One-third is purest character.* It is the beautiful righteousness of the gospel. A beggarly thing when he describes it. In his mind it is no more than the moralist's life of right doing, from which Paul shrank so much, that he hoped he might not be found in it at the judgment day. Gospel righteousness is an immaculate thing. Our righteousness by the side of it is as filthy rags, hence the apostle's cry, "That I may be found in Christ, not having mine own righteousness, but the righteousness of God, which is by faith." Well might we desire the same, for then:

> "Bold shall we stand in that great day,
> For who aught to our charge shall lay;
> While through Christ's blood absolved we are
> From sin's tremendous curse and shame."

> "Jesus Thy blood and righteousness
> Our beauty are our glorious dress
> 'Midst these, in flaming worlds, arrayed,
> With joy shall we lift up our head."

From all this we cannot escape the conclusion that while religion is a system of beliefs, the articles of our faith result in experiences that affect the very center of our being, our affectional nature, not only producing an ethical change but of

The Pentecostal Blessing

necessity firing the entire life with the pure emotion of delight in God. The subjects of grace find *that grace to be glory*, and such glory that the heart bursts with praises to God. It is impossible to accompany Christ from the throne to the manger, and from Bethlehem to Gethsemane, and from the garden to Golgotha, and from Olivet to the seventh heaven and to feel the mystery of His indwelling the believer, without the strong emotion of gratitude and love. Divine praises *will* well up within, and brook no effort of repression, and the house of God will be of all places the seemliest for their expression. Unnatural is that sanctuary service, and those conditions, and that conception of religion which preclude a child of God glorying in his Redeemer. To frown upon emotional religion is clearly not to have the Spirit of Christ, but the spirit of the Pharisees. The Word tells us of an occasion when the whole multitude of disciples began to rejoice and praise God with a loud voice for all the mighty works which they had seen, saying: "Blessed be the King that cometh in the name of the Lord: peace in heaven, and glory in the highest." The Pharisees desired to have the disciples rebuked, but Christ answered and said: "I tell you that if these should hold their peace the stones would immediately cry out." When shall we understand that *praise is never out of order*, that we should bless the Lord at all times, that His praise should continually be in our mouth. "Whoso offereth praise," saith God, "glorifieth Me." "O give thanks unto the Lord for He is good . . . let the *redeemed* of the Lord say so, whom He hath redeemed from the hand of the enemy." Such is the Spirit-filled life that it would sooner cease to breathe than cease to praise.

Perpetually does it say: "Bless the Lord, O my soul: and all that is within me, bless His holy name. Who forgiveth all thine iniquities; who healeth all thy diseases; who redeemeth thy life

Some Misconceptions of the Gospel

from destruction; who crowneth thee with loving kindness and tender mercies. . . . Bless the Lord, ye his angels, that excel in strength, that do His commandments, hearkening to the voice of His word. Bless ye the Lord, all ye His hosts; ye ministers of His that do His pleasure. Bless the Lord, all His works in all places of His dominion."

"Oh for such grace let rocks and hills
Their lasting silence break;
And all harmonious creature tongues
The Saviour's praises speak."

Hallelujah! Hallelujah! Hallelujah!

A third misconception is that the gospel can be realized without spirituality. We have heard various grievously heretical doctrines and pseudo-religious philosophies, each in their own day, described as the masterpiece of Satan, but *we know of nothing that is comparable to the device of worldliness for the damnation of souls*, because it admits of a man being mentally orthodox, while he is morally corrupt and spiritually a cipher. The worldly religious are the hardest people to reach. They believe in the church, support it, are ready to assent to its theological propositions, and they subscribe to the accepted cardinal doctrines of Christianity; but withal, there dwells within them an idolatrous heart. Their devotion is not devotion to God, but to forms and ceremonies connected with His Name, and when through these, with the zest of any non-professor, will yield themselves to the service of self and Satan. Consequently these souls are lost when they have not the remotest suspicion of any such desperate personal condition. Like Herod, who did many things and heard John gladly they nevertheless fail to do *the* thing, the one thing absolutely needful. All their doing in the house of God is profitless, and worse, a snare destroying the possibility of the knowledge of the redemptive work of Christ; for it is written: "If any man love the world, the love of the Father is not in him." Scripture, you note, sweeps clean from the soul the false notion of knowing the love of God, if in the heart be found the love of the world. *The truth of the gospel is after godliness* according to the first verse of Titus I. And according to Titus 2:II, 12, the grace of God that bringeth salvation, is a grace teaching the denial of ungodliness and worldly lusts, and enjoining the life of sobriety, righteousness and godliness. To mix religion and the world is sacrilegious. What fellowship hath righteousness with unrighteousness? What communion hath light with darkness? It is presumption and not faith to claim salvation when the heart refuses and hath no desire to go forth unto Jesus without the camp bearing His reproach. Remember the solemn words in James 4:4: "Ye adulterers and adulteresses, know ye not that friendship with the world is enmity with God. Whosoever will be a friend of the world is an enemy of God." Verily then, "to be carnally minded is death; but to be spiritually minded is life and peace."

A fourth misconception is the notion that the gospel requires supplemental methods for its prosperity at home and abroad. This may not seem to be a vital error in the church of God, but we shall hope to show in the after pages of this book that it is, and the people of God ought to retrace immediately the false steps they have taken in this direction. Very insidiously has this notion worked in the church of God. Did not we all find it prevailing when we were brought into connection with the church, and not being enlightened from the Word and by our teachers, we accepted the system of work in vogue without a question, and formed easily the habit of doing things according to custom. We took for granted that the traditional was the true way. How often we have said it over and over again to ourselves and to one another, "Do not our denominational leaders think so? They ought to know. They are men of piety and wisdom." So we contented ourselves in thinking that all was well; but in this compliance with tradition we have unwittingly yielded to man the headship of the church *which belongs to Christ alone*. It is our solemn conviction for which we can give reasons that a great mistake has been made in the modern church in associating with the office of bishop and elder, functions legislative. The mistake has also been extended to the church itself. She in representing the only true faith in the earth, and receiving the responsibility of a world-wide message, has interpreted that she must devise ways and means to strengthen herself and her influence, and to carry the Word to the ends of the earth, whereas, she has nothing whatever to do with devising ways and means to promote the Lord's glory among men. With the open Bible before us, of apostolic life covering a period of fully half a century, we cannot sympathize with the modern denominational methods of promoting the gospel of Christ. We venture to assert that if churches had not become apostate and worldly there would never have been societies and missionary boards. We find not so much as a hint of these things in New Testament days. The plea cannot be reasonably entered that the church of those days was not fully developed, and that methods were left for after generations to formulate. The church being peculiarly the Lord's own organization He has a care, not only touching the things to be believed but touching the ways of His people's service. *We contend that whatever is essential to the spread*

The Pentecostal Blessing

and growth of the gospel both in doctrine and in method was made known by the great Head of the church through His apostles. Let us be careful about being wiser than the Word in anything. The ways and means for spiritual life and missionary activity have not been left to the wisdom of man, not even to his sanctified common sense that we hear so much about whatever that may mean. If ladies' guilds and young people's societies and men's clubs and boys' brigades and entertainment sociables, and missionary boards are essential to the maintenance and increase of the gospel, why were not these things introduced by the apostles? They are singularly absent from the early church, and what is very noteworthy, more, proportionately, was accomplished for Christ in apostolic time without these appendages than in our day with them. We do not regard as a justification of modern methods the good that has been accomplished by them, because in adopting them we are denying to the Lord Jesus Christ who is the Head of the Church, the all-sufficiency of His ways and means in the accomplishment of His own will. In this we have done a serious wrong to our Lord Jesus Christ. Let the wrong be righted by the faithful of our day. But it may be urged that if the present auxiliaries be overthrown there would be no missionary church. Let it be understood that we grant the necessity of these modern methods in an apostate and worldly church, but suppose we were to dispense with these arms of flesh and each organization become a spiritual body squaring its life and practice by the Word, the result would be that overthrowing the societies within the church and the missionary boards on the outside of the church, the church of Christ would quickly be seen to be all-sufficient without any auxiliaries to carry out the entire revealed will of God in spiritual matters in the earth. This is proven by instances here and there, of which the First New Testament Church of Los Angeles is an illustration. Organized with only about a membership of two hundred and twenty-five, on the principle that the Lord founded but one body of people, and that the church, of which He only is the Head; and distrusting absolutely the wisdom of man for work divine; it exists and flourishes, increasing weekly in numbers, and spiritual strength and influence, without any sub-organizations or the help of missionary boards to fan its missionary life; and ere four months of its life it had laid on God's altar without any personal solicitation, at one service, over three thousand dollars for Christian missions; and before it was six months old had set apart two choice young men of its own membership for independent missionary work in China. Oh! mightily would grow the Word of God and prevail if only the wisdom of man were renounced and the wisdom of God exalted.

CHAPTER 2

Modern Conditions

Let us ask, "what is the condition of the world, and what the condition of the churches of Jesus Christ?" As we look upon the first, the sight is one of lunacy. The people are mad. There is riot in the mind, riot in the heart, riot in the will. Gold is the goal of life; pleasure and fashion the sum of life; and religion the side issue of life, except when it is spiritualism, Christian science (?), millennial dawn, ritualism, Catholicism, and the like. Scripturally described the view is that of the lust of the flesh, the lust of the eye, and the pride of life. Does the reader see the same thing? Perhaps not. He might be looking, and with all honesty, at the myriad spires of the evangelical churches, the costly ecclesiastical, educational and philanthropic plants, the march of civilization in the comity and humanity of modern life, and the arbitration councils of nations. And maybe he is saying, "Herein is the hope of the world. The spirit that these things embody will subdue in time the baser passions, and the infidel philosophies of the race. We are not in the twilight of evening but of morning. Let us believe in the survival and supremacy of all the good influences now shedding their soft and kindly light of dawn across the gloomy firmament." Our reply is simple, and we submit pertinent. We await an answer to it. We will rejoice to take such a view of our age if it can be proven that the truth which gave birth to the churches, and to this march of civilization is not being daily put to dishonour and death, and that, too, by the civilization and churches which owe their very existence to it. It is a fact of history that before Christianity there was no civilization that was a credit to man's moral nature save occasionally Jewish life, and if the civilization of today makes a fair show of ethics what place is it yielding to that religion from whence it has drawn all which it has that is worthy of a boast. The charge which we bring against the world is that it only accepts Christianity's minor moralities. It rejects the entire system of spiritualities. How long, then, will present civilization maintain its moral characteristics if it repudiates the Christian soil in which only it can thrive? Separate a flower from its plant and we know that it will soon cease to retain its bloom and beauty. Likewise will it be with the few fair blossoms of our modern civilization. They are doomed to fade, for our age has no use for the plant from which they have been plucked.

And does our reader point to the omnipresent church life? The situation we admit ought to be splendid in experience and potentially great—radiant with grandest hopes. But it is neither one nor the other. We live in a time when the churches display a great deal of stage scenery. They have comfortable homes, which in many instances are architecturally fine; and if strength be gauged by numbers, they can, united, command for the cause they represent any adverse circumstance that may threaten their life. Their internal construction challenges improvement. If virtue be in up-to-date methods the latest are being applied

Modern Conditions

to their work. If aesthetics are necessary to win the ear and eye and heart of man these are not lacking, for, art in the pulpit, art in the pew, and art in the choir-loft are in evidence to a superlative degree. With this wealthy resource, what are the facts in achievements. *Achievement, remember, must be determined by the purpose of the church in the mind* of God. The organization being the only organization God founded for the expression of His will, religiously considered, then its results are not according to appearances and popular estimates, but just so many and no more than those which correspond *to the purpose of its life in the intention of God.* For the sake of clearness let us put in table form the church of today by the side of the church of the Scriptures, then we shall see at a glance whether it be of God, and whether it can work out a millennium for the world, as many believe it will do, and, as many believe it is already doing.

The Church of Today	The Church of the Scriptures
	(By which is meant not the church in history, except the Pentecostal church, but the church according to the plan of God.)
Has various heads and masters.	Just one—the Lord Jesus Christ. (Col. I:18.)
Has various creeds.	Just one—the faith of our Lord Jesus Christ. (Jude 3.)
Without spiritual freedom. Fettered by forms, ceremonies and customs. Capable of human	Extraordinary. Unaccountable by man. In humiliation and suffering, yet a thing of mighty power, confounding the world by its unearthly life and a grievous anxiety to civil authorities. Turning the

The Pentecostal Blessing

The Church of Today	The Church of the Scriptures
e x p l a n a t i o n . Everything about its religious life ordinary and commonplace. Believes the day of miracles is past. Any influence it has is obtained at the expense of compromises.	world upside down amid all the opposition of the world. Doing the promised greater things of Christ; in a word, supernatural. (John 14:12; Read the Acts of the Apostles, I Cor. 12:4-11.)
Relies upon the natural and cultivated gifts of its preachers and choirs for its welfare.	Behold your calling, brethren, that not many wise after the flesh, not many mighty, not many noble are called, but God chose the foolish things of the world, that He might put to shame them that are wise; and God chose the weak things of the world, that he might put to shame the things that are strong; and the base things of the world, and the things that are despised, did God choose; yea, and the things that are not, that He might bring to nought things that are: that no flesh should glory before God. He that glorieth let him glory in the Lord. (I Cor. 1:26, 29, 31.)
Lives for the praise of men.	Not in the way of eye service as men pleasers, but as servants of Christ, doing

Modern Conditions

The Church of Today	The Church of the Scriptures
Worldly.	the will of God from the heart; with good will doing service unto the Lord, and not unto men. We speak not as pleasing men, but God who proveth our hearts. For neither at any time were we found using words of flattery, as ye know; nor a cloak of covetousness, God is witness; nor seeking glory of men, neither from you nor from others. We make it our aim . . . to be well pleasing unto him. For we must all be made manifest before the judgment seat of Christ. (Ephes. 6:6, 7; I Thess. 2:4, 5, 6; 2 Cor. 5:9.) Be not unequally yoked with unbelievers: for what fellowship have righteousness and iniquity? or what communion hath light with darkness? and what concord hath Christ with Belial? or what portion hath a believer with an unbeliever? And what agreement hath a temple of God with idols? for we are a temple of the living God; even as God said, I will dwell in them, and walk in them; and I will be their God, and they shall be my people. Wherefore, come ye out from among them, and be ye separate, saith the Lord, and touch no unclean

The Pentecostal Blessing

The Church of Today	The Church of the Scriptures
	thing; and I will receive you, and will be to you a Father; and ye shall be to me sons and daughters, saith the Lord Almighty. Having therefore these promises, beloved, let us cleanse ourselves from all defilement of the flesh and spirit, perfecting holiness in the fear of God. (2 Cor. 6:14–18; 2 Cor. 7:1.)
Thirsts for a worldly good time.	The kingdom of God is not meat and drink, but righteousness, and peace, and joy in the Holy Ghost. Put ye on the Lord Jesus Christ, and make not provision for the flesh, to fulfill the lusts thereof. That thou mayest know how men ought to behave themselves in the house of God, which is the church of the living God, the pillar and the ground of the truth. (Rom. 14:17; Rom. 13:14; 1 Tim. 3:15.)
Respecter of persons and bribed by Simon Magus, who obtains influence and office.	My brethren, hold not the faith of our Lord Jesus Christ, the Lord of Glory, with respect of persons. For if there come into your assembly a man with a gold ring, in fine clothing, and there come in also a poor man in vile clothing; and ye have regard to him that weareth the fine clothing, and say, Sit thou here in a good

~ 48 ~

Modern Conditions

The Church of Today	The Church of the Scriptures
	place; and ye say to the poor man, Stand thou there, or sit under my footstool; do ye not make distinctions among yourselves, and become judges with evil thoughts? Hearken, my beloved brethren, did not God choose them that are poor as to the world, rich in faith, and heirs of the kingdom, which he promised to them that love him? . . . if ye have respect of persons ye commit sin. When Simon saw that through the laying on of the apostle's hands the Holy Spirit was given, he offered them money, saying, Give me also this power, that on whomsoever I lay my hands, he may receive the Holy Spirit. But Peter said unto him, Thy silver perish with thee because thou hast thought to obtain the gift of God with money. Thou hast neither part nor lot in this matter: for thy heart is not right before God. Repent therefore of this thy wickedness, and pray the Lord, if perhaps the thought of thy heart shall be forgiven thee. For I see that thou art in the gall of bitterness, and in the bond of iniquity. (James 2:1–6, 9; Acts 8:18, 23.)

The Pentecostal Blessing

The Church of Today	The Church of the Scriptures
Quarrelsome, contentious, jealous, place hunting, position seeking; and these things are as true of the ministry as of the pew.	For I say, through the grace that was given me, to every man that is among us, not to think of himself more highly than he ought to think. In love of the brethren be tenderly affectioned one to another, in honor preferring one another. Be clothed with humility. Be of the same mind, having the same love, being of one accord, of one mind; doing nothing through faction or through vainglory, but in lowliness of mind each counting other better than himself. Do all things without murmurings and questionings; that ye may become blameless and harmless children of God without blemish in the midst of a crooked and perverse generation, among whom ye are seen as lights in the world. Put on therefore, as God's elect, holy and beloved, a heart of compassion, kindness, lowliness, meekness, long suffering, forbearing one another, and forgiving each other; if any man have a complaint against any, even as the Lord forgave you, so also do ye: and above all these things put on love which is the

Modern Conditions

The Church of Today	The Church of the Scriptures
	bond of perfectness. And let the peace of Christ rule in your hearts, to the which also ye were called in one body. (Rom. 12:3, 10; I Peter 5:5; Phil. 2:2, 3, 14, 15; Col. 3:12–15.)
Says it cannot live without sin.	My little children, I write unto you that ye sin not. As children of obedience, not fashioning yourselves according to your former lusts in the time of your ignorance: but like as he who called you is holy, be ye yourselves also holy in all manner of living; because it is written, ye shall be holy; for I am holy. That ye may be sincere, and void of offense unto the day of Christ. Walk worthily of the Lord unto all pleasing, and the God of peace himself sanctify you wholly; and may your spirit, and soul, and body, be preserved entire, without blame unto the coming of our Lord Jesus Christ. (I John 2:1; I Peter 1:14, 15, 16; Phil. 1:10; Col. 1:10; I Thess. 5:23.)
Aims at a comfortable and inoffensive profession of Christ.	If any man would come after me, let him deny himself and take up his cross and follow me; for whosoever would save his life shall lose it; and whosoever

The Church of Today	The Church of the Scriptures
	will lose his life for my sake and the gospel's shall find it. Let us therefore go forth unto him without the camp bearing his reproach. (Mark 8:34, 35; Heb. 13:13. Go ye into all the world and preach the gospel to every creature.
Yields a preference to education rather than to works of evangelization.	Go ye and disciple all the nations, baptizing them in the name of the Father, and of the Son, and of the Holy Spirit: teaching them (for which a scholastic university training is unnecessary; see I John 2:20, 27) to observe all things whatsoever I command you. They . . . went everywhere preaching the word. (Mark 16:15; Matt. 28:19, 20; Acts 8:4.)
Doing many things which preclude its undivided attention upon and effectiveness in the great work of its life. Boasting of what it does. Glorying in and striving to build	In service pre-eminently at work spreading the gospel of salvation by a crucified Christ. (Read the Book of Acts.) When ye shall have done all the things which are commanded you, say, We are unprofitable servants; we have done that which was our duty to do. (Luke 17:10.) Whatsoever ye do, in word or deed, do all in the name of the Lord Jesus.

Modern Conditions

The Church of Today	The Church of the Scriptures
up denominationalism.	That they may all be one, even as thou, Father, art in me, and I in Thee. That they also may be in us: that the world may believe that thou didst send me. (Col. 3:17; John 17:21.)
Filled with societies.	Not a trace of auxiliaries.
The work of the minister: To discuss the topics of the day, to produce word painting sermons, to give stereopticon and other lectures, to make society calls, to shine in social functions, to play the funny and humorous man, to interest people in the church.	The work of the minister: The perfecting of the saints . . . the building up of the body of Christ: till we all attain unto the unity of the faith, and of the knowledge of the Son of God, unto a full grown man, unto the measure of the stature of the fulness of Christ. Take heed unto yourselves and to all the flock in which the Holy Spirit hath made you bishops to feed the church of God, which he purchased with his own blood. Christ . . . whom we proclaim, admonishing every man and teaching every man in all wisdom, that we may present every man perfect in Christ, whereunto I labor also. I charge thee in the sight of God, and of Christ Jesus, who shall judge the living and the dead, and by his appearing and his kingdom: preach the word; be

The Church of Today	The Church of the Scriptures
	urgent in season, out of season; reprove, rebuke, exhort, with all long-suffering and teaching. (Ephes. 4:12, 13; Acts 20:28; Col. 1:2:8, 29; 2 Tim. 4:1, 2.)
Pulpit themes: Minor moralities; principles of reformation; human philosophies of life; patriotism; the poets; politics; men of today and yesterday; science, and occasionally the gospel.	Pulpit themes: All spiritual: the mystery of godliness. God manifest in the flesh; the depravity and lost estate of man out of Christ; Christ and Him crucified; justification by faith; the Spirit-filled life; sanctification; the second coming of Christ, and all the great truths of the revealed will of God.
Prayerless, notwithstanding its prayer meetings.	Pray without ceasing. Praying in the Holy Ghost. In everything by prayer and supplication, with thanksgiving, let your requests be made known before God. Continue steadfastly in prayer and watch in the same with thanksgiving. (I Thess. 5:17; Ephes. 6:18; Phil. 4:6; Col. 4:2.)

This table is its own commentary, and we do not hesitate to conclude that there can be no bettering of the time religiously until a change takes place in the house of God. As a

Modern Conditions

people, supposedly of the Lord, we are in this world to call men to repentance, but it is time to close the doors, and call one another to repentance and fasting and prayer. It is a time to weep between the porch and the altar. The house needs cleaning. The people of God must get rid of their sins, the traditions of their elders, their man-made systems of religion, their denominational love and glorying, so dishonoring to God, their carnal mind with all its belongings, and exchange their wisdom for the mind of Christ, their strength for his power, and their activity for the will of God, and then enthrone the Lord Head of His own house. Until this is done it will not be well with us, neither will our life be a power over the world. The people of God for the most part today are playing the part of the legerdemain before men, and men know it. They pretend to be what they are not, God's representatives, and men know it. They propose to them what they have not themselves, the higher life, and men know it. They set forth for men a better service, but they themselves stand for only the service of refined selfishness, and men know it. The world sees in the face of the church but a reflection of itself, and those of their number who cast in their lot with the church do but repeat its folly, for while they take up with the fear of the Lord, they still go on serving the gods of the creature.

CHAPTER 3

The Explanation

Coming fresh from the study of the table our exclamation must be, what a discrepancy! Can we look at the church of to-day and the church idealized in the Scriptures, which was at one time in concrete illustration in the earth, and not have great searchings of heart before the Lord? Why the unlikeness and contradiction, and what a shame that the present day church should presume to represent the Lord even by name when its life is no more as the pattern laid down in the Word than a child's first writing is like the copperplate. There is a reason for this serious and deplorable discrepancy. Shall we not try to find it. If we say that the ministry is largely responsible and back of the ministry the theological schools of the land we have only stated a part of the truth. It is true that the grievous situation is not to be wondered at when there is but little spiritual truth taught in our evangelical churches, and when the great things after conversion are set forth as union with the visible church, and union with young people's and ladies' and men's organized follies; and serving on committees, some of which play at religion, and others engender a spirit contrary to religion, and others yet again exist in name only, for they rarely, if ever, do any work; and when church ideals are sociables, literary evenings, musicales, organ recitals, raising money by worldly expedients, and a fleshly affability which flatters human nature with a view of commanding organic success. Such a state of things plainly declares that many hirelings are in the pulpit, that many men are preachers professionally, instead of by the call of God, that many men are man-made ministers instead of God's anointed.

If pulpits are filled with men without spiritual qualifications, how can the church be taught the things of God? The poor church of God is afflicted with blind ministers, and it's a case of the blind leading the blind. The church is overrun with a spirit foreign to its true life. Where only the Lord's anointed should stand, the traditionalist too often is seen, the man who magnifies creature religion, who lives for carnal display and denominational glory, the time server that makes merchandise of the house of God. Oh church of the living God thou art fallen! Thy friends are thy foes. Thy love is human not divine. In works thou servest not God, but the unworthy ends of man's selfish and sinful ambitions.

This state of things should make us enquire concerning the things vital to the house of God. To say the least it is unnatural for the church not to express in its organized life that which is infinitely superior to the life of clubs and lodges. The church ought to be more than a congregation of human elements, and must be, and indeed is, if it be of God. We have a right to look to the church and to all individual Christians for the expression of a supernatural life. The supernatural is their natural state. The people of God do not come into the precious relationship of privilege by merely subscribing to certain articles of faith. To be the people of God is to be in eternal union with God

The Explanation

Himself. If God therefore be missing from our experience, we are not of His house, and we have committed the sin of sacrilege in joining ourselves to His people.

It is God the Holy Ghost who creates and sustains a Christian, and also who creates and sustains the church; and this being so, we must turn to Him for Christians that are Christians indeed, and for a church in the earth that shall illustrate among men the way of divine life and service. Having failed to honour *Him*, we have failed in all things vital to Christianity, and therefore vital to a true representation of the church of Jesus Christ. Because we have not given to the Holy Ghost the place assigned Him in the church by the Scriptures we are affected with the higher criticism, and worldliness, supplemental and unnecessary methods, superfluous organization for the maintenance and spread of the Faith, and men of a dwarfed Christian stature with their narrow sympathies and circumscribed view of the gospel. None of these are possible where the Holy Spirit is supreme. Let us study Him and get back to God, and to power, and to a position where we can throw the fear of God across the people's vision, and bless the world.

Our theoretical orthodoxy must be enlarged and translated into an every-day experience. Scripture calls us to the worship of a Triune God—Father, Son *and Holy Ghost*. Practically considered modern Christian worship is very defective, vitally, fundamentally defective. It is a worship of the Father and the Son, but scarcely a worship of the Holy Ghost. Shall we not understand that God is not truly worshiped until He is recognized as Triune, and adoration be given *equally* to the three Persons? If the Holy Spirit were acknowledged indeed as God, a radically different state of things would be prevailing in Christendom.

The Pentecostal Blessing

The Spirit honoured in the glory of His Godhead means the Spirit of God revealing the glory of God among men. The two go together. The return of the church to the worship of the Holy Ghost *will be the return to the church of the long lost glory of God*. Therefore, the great truth to be pressed to the attention and hearts of the professing people of God today, is the truth of the divine Spirit. Every one of us who are jealous for the honour of the Lord, the purity and prosperity of the church of Jesus Christ, must make everything of this subject for the time being. It is THE subject of subjects for the people of God. We must keep this to the front. It must be our daily declaration until every Christian becomes solemnly affected by it. The Holy Spirit is a *Person*, the Holy Spirit is *God*, the Holy Spirit is *the third Person of the Trinity*, the Holy Spirit must be worshipped, and *only through* the Holy Spirit are Father and Son *revealed*. Let Zion but be engaged with this truth and the profoundest awakening will result. She will be filled with a glory that will light up the whole earth. It is this that will start revival fires in every place in the world. As a proof, I have but to cite again the First New Testament Church of Los Angeles. The secret of the profound spiritual movement there is in the fact that that church has recovered the shamefully obscured and long buried truth of the Holy Spirit, and is opening its heart for the embodiment of Him. Do strangers who visit it ask, "Why is the glory of God in the place?" The answer returned them, brief and simple, is "We are worshiping the Holy Ghost." Note that, "*worshiping*" the Holy Ghost, that is to say, adoring Him as God, but more, yielding the place that is given to Him by the Scriptures and given to Him by the Father and the Son. He is enthroned as the executive. They seek to give way to His office work. They desire Him to speak and work as He wills in His own house. They wish Him to be the

The Explanation

Sovereign Administrator, and themselves His servants. And this is just what is signified in the true worship of God.

Would the churches everywhere have a revival? They must honour the Holy Spirit. Many are the churches that are praying for a revival, but some of them know not for what they are asking. If God were to answer their prayers they would refuse the revival when it came. How ignorantly the professing people of God as a whole think of a revival. Have you thought of what is inevitable in a true revival? This much for certain, *the destruction of man's authority in the house of* God. But this is the last thing that man will yield. A true revival is the exaltation of the Holy Spirit in the church. A true revival is the sovereign workings of that authority. Against those sovereign workings religious man is in perpetual rebellion. Are the churches asking for a revival? If it be of God when it comes it will be Wales over again. But a Welsh revival is not what many churches can stand, bound as they are to the traditional life, to creeds, man-made systems and notions of service. The modern church is afflicted with creature religion which will be swept away in a revival from God. Oh for a general crying out for an exaltation of our Lord:

> "Let *men* before Him fall.
> Bring forth the royal diadem,
> And crown *Him* Lord of all."

CHAPTER 4

The Pentecostal Blessing

To express our view point we will quote the language of Article IV in the constitutional statement of the First New Testament Church of Los Angeles. It defines clearly our position. That formula of spiritual belief reads as follows:

"We hold that it is the duty and privilege of the believer to know the Holy Spirit as 'the promise of the Father,' (Acts I:4) elsewhere spoken of as 'The Gift,' (Acts 2:38) *an experience distinct from regeneration*. The disciples knew not the Holy Spirit as 'the promise of the Father,' or in other words as 'The Gift *until the day of Pentecost*, therefore we speak of the Spirit as 'The Pentecostal Blessing,' necessary to the believer's sanctification, his knowledge of the fullness of God, and his anointing for service."

While the truth here formulated is laying hold of hearts today in a way unknown a few years ago, we note a great zeal in some quarters to combat the Scripturalness of this position by contending that every person knows the Spirit in conversion. But this is not the issue raised on the subject we are treating. We also say that no soul can be a Christian without the Spirit, for it is plainly written: "If any man have not the Spirit

The Pentecostal Blessing

of Christ he is none of His." In the advocacy of the Pentecostal Blessing we maintain that the blessing known in conversion is not the blessing known in Pentecost. *Pentecost involves a second great work of grace.* We say, not that it is necessarily removed from the time of conversion, but that it is *distinct*. It is possible to know the blessing the very same day, and according to the solitary recorded instance in Scripture (Acts 10:44-48) it is not impossible of knowledge in the moments of the quickening of the soul unto eternal life. However, and underscore it much in your mind, Pentecost and Regeneration are not one and the same thing. If so most professing Christians would be in a sad plight, for they have never known with Cornelius, the Holy Ghost falling upon them, and would be doomed to continue in the anomalous conditions of their present experience until released by death. Regeneration is simply life. Pentecost is the *fullness* and the *abundance of life*. Even as in nature when we were born, we were babes, and all that could be said of us was that we were alive, so it is the usual phenomenon in grace. When a person is born again he is a babe in his every spiritual appearance. Fullness comes not in the new birth but subsequently. Acts 2:38 supplies us with an illustration. When did Peter say that the sin-convicted should receive the gift? The blessing was to be theirs after repentance and baptism, for observe, the Scripture of the Pentecost begins with a copulative conjunction. Look at what precedes it: "*Repent and be baptized* every one of you in the name of Jesus Christ for the remission of sins, *and* ye shall receive the gift of the Holy Ghost."

The knowledge of Jesus by the hundred and twenty that met in the upper room did not involve Pentecost. Some of them at least had known Jesus for many years. Pentecost came to them not when they were called to be His disciples, but as a

The Pentecostal Blessing

result of their experience of Jesus. Pentecost was not their introduction to Christian experience. It came to develop, strengthen and expand what they already had. This is ever the mission of Pentecost. Pentecost is never the beginning of grace in the soul; *it is the feeder of grace previously received.* Our first blessing is regeneration. *Our second blessing in the purpose of God is Pentecost.* And let me say, the second is as real as the first, and as important to the believer, as regeneration is to the sinner. Regeneration should be succeeded by Pentecost. Has it been in you, dear reader? If the only Christian experience that you have had is the new birth, then Pentecost awaits you. There is something more than the act of union with Christ. There is a growing knowledge within the soul of all that is involved in that union. Do not take up the unworthy attitude of many by saying that you have comprehended the gospel simply because you have believed on the Lord Jesus Christ. The gospel cannot be measured by the mind of man. A very little of it is known at the new birth. Believe me, nay, believe the Word, it is not a Chinese shoe. If tradition and church beliefs have narrowed and circumscribed the truth of God into such a shoe, imprisoning your feet, then throw it away, and become shod with the preparation of the real gospel: "I am come," says Christ, "that they might have life, and that they might have it more abundantly."

> "Have you on the Lord believed?
> Still there's more to follow;
> Of His grace have you received?
> Still there's more to follow;
> Oh, the grace the Father shows!
> Still there's more to follow!

The Pentecostal Blessing

Freely He His grace bestows,
Still there's more to follow!"

"Have you felt the Spirit's power?
Still there's more to follow;
Falling like the mighty shower?
Still there's more to follow;
Oh, the power the Spirit shows!
Still there's more to follow!
Freely He His power bestows!
Still there's more to follow!"

"More and more, more and more,
Always more to follow!
Oh, His matchless, boundless love!
Still there's more to follow!"

Oh, believer, be ever going in for more and *more*, and MORE, and MORE.

One of the means used in discouraging souls to seek their Pentecost is to advance the thought that Pentecost was a blessing bestowed ten days after the ascension and was given once for all. This, we would remind the reader, is but a half truth. Pentecost in the sense of the Holy Spirit coming from heaven did take place ten days after our Lord's ascension, and was not repeated. The Holy Ghost in coming to this world came to stay throughout the dispensation. Since that wonderful day of His advent He has never returned. He is no temporary gift to the church. He will be with us until Jesus comes, and then after that also, for it is written: "The Father shall give you another Comforter, that he may abide with you forever." But now let not

The Pentecostal Blessing

unbelief say there is but one Pentecost, and that happened in apostolic times, for the facts of history declare otherwise. In the eighth of Acts there was a Samaritan Pentecost; in the tenth of Acts there was a Roman Pentecost; in the nineteenth of Acts there was a Grecian Pentecost. Neither of them occurred at the same time, and each of them was subsequent to the Jerusalem Pentecost. We have not to rely wholly upon New Testament history for light upon a matter of so great a moment, for the church since that day has known many a Pentecost, and one is being experienced at this very time in the principality of Wales. Let these facts awaken our expectations. This world has yet to know a latter rain, exceeding the moderately former rain, for it is written: "I will pour out my Spirit upon all flesh," a Scripture that has never yet been fulfilled. It is the way of God to keep the best wine until the last and while not in our day are all flesh likely to know the descent of the Spirit, yet, as this dispensation opened with a remarkable effusion of the Spirit upon believers, may we not confidently look for a remarkable effusion of the Spirit upon believers whose lot is cast in the closing hours of the dispensation. Such an effusion is absolutely necessary just prior to our Lord's second advent; for the Lamb's bride will make herself ready for the bridegroom and this is not possible without the Pentecostal power of the Spirit. And even as the coming of the Spirit in the opening days of this dispensation resulted in numerous conversions so may we look for a great ingathering during the last Pentecost of the dispensation. God has a larger grace for this world than it has ever known. It is coming! It is coming! I hear His chariot wheels. There is a sound of abundance of rain. How conditions in our midst are resembling the Jerusalem of Peter's day. Los Angeles is a modern Jerusalem from the standpoint of inhabitants. Of old were there not Parthians, and Medes, and Elamites and the dwellers in Mesopotamia and in Judea, and Cappadocia, in Pontus and Asia, Phrygia and Pamphylia, in Egypt and in the parts of Libya about Cyrene, and strangers of Rome, Jews and proselytes, Cretes and Arabians? If we are to conclude from the cosmopolitan character of American life, God is preparing the mightiest Pentecost ever known; for here on a gigantic scale is the world epitomized. Here is every continent. Here are all nations. Here are north, east, south and west of the world congregated, and what for? Commerce? Politics? Nay, the gospel! That men may hear everywhere in their own tongue the wonderful works of God. Oh, there is coming a mighty upheaval, a spiritual revolution, upon a phenomenal scale, in which the heavens and the earth shall answer the one to the other. Yes, for:

> "The God that lived at Pentecost
> Is just the same today."

"God hath spoken once; twice have I heard this that power belongeth unto God." He saith: "Write the vision and make it plain upon tables, that he may run that readeth it, for the vision is yet for an appointed time, but at the end it shall speak and not lie, though it tarry wait for it because it will surely come." "I will overturn, and overturn, and overturn." He hath promised, saying: "Yet once more I shake not the earth only, but also heaven." "And the Lord whom ye seek shall suddenly come to his temple." Oh, let us be on the tiptoe of expectancy, "for when the day of Pentecost was fully come, and they were all with one accord in one place, SUDDENLY there came a sound from heaven as of a rushing mighty wind, and it filled all the house where they were sitting." I love to think of the suddenness of

The Pentecostal Blessing

the Spirit's coming. That, beloved, is how He is coming to us. It will be like lightning from the skies. It will be in an unlikely moment to multitudes. Think of the revival under Jonathan Edwards. He came one day to his pulpit with a closely written manuscript on the text: *"Their feet shall slide in due time."* His subject, *"A sinner in the hands of an angry God."* He began reading it—think of it—and being near-sighted he held his manuscript close to his eyes. There were no gesticulations. He stood quietly in the pulpit reading, but as he read, Pentecost came, the people trembled, were terror-stricken with conviction. The scene was strange and sensational. Some fell to the ground, some swooned, some groaned, and others clutched the pillars of the church, lest—to use their own expression—"they should slide into hell." Oh, God can bring His blessings instantly. He has but to speak and it is done. Suddenly among us, He will say: "Let there be light," and there shall be light. The Lord whom ye seek shall suddenly come to His temple.

But, Pentecost is personal as well as congregational. Have you particularly noticed this? In Acts 2:3 we read: "And there appeared unto them tongues parting asunder, like as of fire; and it sat upon EACH ONE OF THEM." Pentecost was not an event only for the Lord's people considered as an assembly. Not one in the company was omitted. Every one of the hundred and twenty came in for the blessing. PENTECOST IS FOR THE INDIVIDUAL. Therefore, we read in one Scripture: "Saul, the Lord, even Jesus that appeared unto thee in the way as thou camest, that thou mightest receive thy sight *and be filled with the Holy Ghost.*" In the house of Cornelius, while Peter was preaching, the Holy Ghost fell on *all,* observe that, will you, *all* them which heard the Word. At Ephesus *each* of the twelve disciples received the baptism of the Holy Ghost. And the characters whom

The Pentecostal Blessing

God baptizes are remarkable. Here and there one like Paul of culture and talents, but more often than not He lays hold of the rough and uncouth, the lowly and nobodies of the world. The Spirit, like the wind, goeth where He listeth. What saith the Scripture: "Ye see your calling brethren, how that not many wise men after the flesh, not many mighty, not many noble are called. But God hath chosen the foolish things of the world to confound the wise, and God hath chosen the weak things of the world to confound those that are mighty, and base things of the world, and things which are despised, hath God chosen, yea, and things which are not, to bring to naught things that are."

Pentecost awaits those whom, because of the earthliness of their vessel can demonstrate that the excellency of their power is not of man but of God.

This personal blessing is unquestionably from above, and is the sum of all our need. It is not an endowment of nature but a gift of grace. It is the promise of the *Father.* Man is not able to bestow it. It cannot be commanded by his resourceful genius. It is that which comes down from a height above the reach of the creature. *No set of men can form a trust and corner it.* It is not denominational, and more than interdenominational. It is the heritage of all whom the Lord our God shall call, and given direct from God. Consider the descriptive words of Pentecost Acts 1:8. "Ye shall receive power after that the Holy Ghost *is come upon you.*" Joel 2:28. "I"—note that, it is God who is speaking—"I will pour out my Spirit upon all flesh." It is the *ascended Jesus,* spoken of by Peter in Acts 2:33 as having *shed forth* that which the people were seeing and hearing. Over in Acts 8:16 it is said: "As yet He was fallen *upon* none of them." Over in Acts 10:44 it is written: "The Holy Ghost *fell* on all them." Over in Acts 19:6: "The Holy Ghost came on them "

The Pentecostal Blessing

Perhaps the reader will here say, "But is not the Gift described as a filling?" Yes, that is the effect of Pentecost. The *cause* is the baptism, the coming down, the pouring forth from on high of the Spirit. Oh, have you known this "down-draught" of the Spirit of God. It is our necessity as individuals and as churches. How vain for the people of God to think and act as if they can get along without the Holy Ghost as *the Gift*. He is the supreme need. What are the life and work of God's people? Far, far away indeed from that conception which so many people seem to have. Look at organized religious life today. Of what does it consist? On the part of the heads of the churches, the cherishing of creeds, the building up of denominations, attending to the things of traditional religion, a great show of the flesh. The phenomenon in the body of the membership is that of worldliness, and the play of evil passions. Young people for the most part only identify themselves with the church because of the sociables, the worldly, good times they might have. Such a life is not the life of a true church of Jesus Christ. Our true life is of God, and for God, but how can we know such a life unless we have the Holy Ghost as the Gift. Religion is spiritual, therefore is dependent upon the Spirit of God. Religion is the working out of the will of God in the creature, but the will of God is never expressed apart from the operations of the Spirit. It is He who works in us to will and to do of His good pleasure. Vain, then, is all this man-made system of life and service which afflicts most modern churches. Vain also the thought that man can bring anything to pass in the progress of the truth in the kingdom of God. Churches that are on the lookout for men to bring true prosperity to pass in their midst are sinning against the Lord. Never will our fellow men be converted by fine architectural houses of worship, never by aesthetic classical music, never by oratorical fireworks, never by a self-seeking officialism, never by permitting sacrilegious hands to touch the sacred work of the church, never by permitting a society life in the pews. These are the chariots and horses of Egypt.

The Holy Ghost! The Holy Ghost!! The Holy Ghost!!!— Oh, I wish I could ring the truth into every preacher's ear, and into the ears of every church member throughout the world— The Holy Ghost, not our genius; The Holy Ghost, not our culture; The Holy Ghost, not our money; The Holy Ghost, and not man, The Holy Ghost is the sum and substance of our need; for Christ having died and risen again, all that is now needed is the power of the Holy Ghost to deliver souls from death and bondage, and to defeat the devil, and to bring the religion of heaven upon the earth. There are many things that are in evidence today in the churches, that are a hindrance instead of a help. To-wit, man's wisdom, man's scheming, man's organizations, man's plans and pretty theories, man's supplements of the will of God. The Lord is waiting upon His people to bless the world. He is wanting a ready people, but our readiness consists, not in our activities, but in our silencing of the flesh life. We must come to the place where we are nothing, and where we can do nothing, and when we are there God will send a mighty deluge of divine grace and baptize the earth with the blessings of heaven. Was it not so of old? Of what account were the apostles without the power of the Holy Ghost? "Tarry ye, then, until ye be endued with power from on high."

CHAPTER 5

The Magnificence of Pentecost

In the Pentecostal Blessing we have discovered a gold mine of unsearchable riches. You may give reins to your hopes. Boundless expectations are justified, for the yield is immeasurable. This is verily so. It cannot be otherwise. Because, first, it consists of a Person, and one who is equal to take the place of Christ. And, second, it consists of one who is no less than the third person of the Adorable Trinity. And, third, it consists of all that is involved in the sovereign workings of the Holy Ghost as "the Gift," as the "promise of the Father," indwelling us. Pentecost in all its reaches must, then, necessarily, be a marvelous mercy. No one can exaggerate, no one can even do justice in describing its greatness and glory. Christ in declaring the expediency of His return to heaven, promised not to leave His people orphans. They should have, said He, "Another Comforter." Now the provision to be adequate, to meet every want, and to satisfy every desire, must be a Comforter the equal of Himself. If not, the substitute proposed could be no compensation for the loss. The need of Christ' s people is not that some one should step into the place of Christ, but that He who succeeds to Christ's place on earth shall really fill Christ's place,

The Pentecostal Blessing

be Christ's equal, rendering equal service. What Christian has not looked wistfully back over those three years of the Twelve with Christ? Who has not in an infantile state of grace, sighed for the bodily presence of Jesus Christ? Who has not, in some great sorrow, exclaimed, "If Thou wert only here as in the days of Thy flesh, if only my arms might be thrown around Thy neck, if only I might sob out the grief of my heart upon Thy bosom, if only I might tell Thee of sufferings hard to endure, the living deaths, what solace and relief would I know for all my troubles. *But lo! some of us have known a moment when we made the discovery, sweet and precious, that that other Comforter is an all-satisfying portion.* And such is the truth, that we cannot think of anything that Jesus can be to His disciples by His bodily presence, but what in His absence that other Comforter supplies the lack. In fact, He is more to us, in some things, than the physical Christ was to the Twelve. The Holy Ghost fills every void and places upon our brow the very crown of life.

The Comforter, which Christ and the Father have sent to the earth, is Their equal, for He is a Person in the Godhead, and being so, is very God of very God. The Gift is not an influence, a mere inspiration, but unquestionably a Person. Never let us degrade the Holy Spirit by calling Him "It." The authorized version of Romans 8:16 may seem to warrant the conclusion for there we read: "The Spirit itself beareth witness," but, if you will read the revision you will see that a change has been made from the impersonal to the personal. Grammatically the authorized version is correct, theologically not so. Had the earlier translators compared Scripture with Scripture upon this subject, they would have done as the revisers, and have given us "the Spirit Himself," for while in the Greek the word for spirit is neuter, here is a remarkable thing to observe, that our Lord

The Magnificence of Pentecost

Jesus Christ in speaking of the Spirit, violates the rules of grammar, in declaring the true nature of the Spirit. Though spirit is neuter, Christ uses the masculine nominative in telling us of the Spirit of God. Consider this, that our Lord says of the Spirit, "*He* abideth with you, *He* shall teach you all things, *He* shall guide you into all truth, *He* shall glorify me, *He* shall declare unto you things that are to come."

Truly we are not left orphans in the world. The Comforter is a Person, even the Most High God. Oh! how great this Pentecostal grace. Grammar is wrecked to speak its greatness. In Pentecost we are united with God Himself, and what a blessing, and that a present blessing.

> "Oh, spread the tidings round, wherever man is found,
> Wherever human hearts and human woes abound;
> Let every Christian tongue proclaim the joyful sound;
> The Comforter has come.
>
> Lo! the great King of kings, with healing in His wings,
> To every captive soul a full deliverance brings;
> And thro' the vacant cells the song of triumph rings:
> The Comforter has come."

"And ye shall receive the gift of the Holy Ghost, for the promise is to all that are afar off, even as many as the Lord our God shall call."

In fullness, *the Pentecostal Blessing is an extraordinary manifestation of the Spirit*. Think of the symbols setting forth the phenomenon of the original Pentecost. "There came from Heaven the sound as of a rushing mighty wind. And there appeared unto them tongues parting asunder, as of fire." Wind and fire are used

The Pentecostal Blessing

to describe the event. Expressive symbols. The Holy Spirit in Pentecostal effusion is a sensational blessing. Dry bones cannot remain dry when He is poured forth. The stillness of death and the grave is broken wherever He comes. He is the Spirit of life, the Spirit of power, the Spirit of fire. How have you conceived of religion? As mere statements to be believed, as quiet church-going, as measured forms and ceremonies? Religion is a thing of the Spirit of God. It is the coming of God among men, in men, upon men. Can His coming have but ordinary effects? Should not we look for surprises? May we not expect a mighty stir? A rushing wind moves things, and fire burns and flames. This we know, get the two together, unite the rushing, mighty wind and the blazing fire, and what can withstand them? Wind and fire will consume a city, and destroy a forest.

In the original Pentecost this Wind filled all the room where they were sitting, and the tongues parting asunder, and sitting upon each of them, gave them wonderful power of speech-the very utterance of the Spirit. Lo, this is the heritage of the people of God. He means them to be a mighty people in the earth; but they are far from this now. What is their life and service as compared with the scene in the second of Acts? Mean, petty, ordinary, commonplace! Present day people of God, for the most part, cringe and fear and compromise when loyalty to the truth and the work of God are involved.

They lack the majesty and heavenliness of the Spirit-built life. The world buys them, circumscribes them, dictates to them, laughs at them, scorns them, masters them, patronizes them. And why? Because they are without their Pentecost, and not until they get it will they be fair as the moon, clear as the sun, and terrible as an army with banners. With Pentecost, fear falls upon every soul. The church becomes a mighty

The Magnificence of Pentecost

power. Pentecost is God, God, God everywhere in the midst. And where He is there must be life and fire. Oh, my Christian reader, consider then the experience, below which we should never live. "He shall baptize you in the Holy Ghost and in fire." God means exactly what He says. When we live in weakness we are not living in the will of God. God intends us to be filled with life, with power, with fire, and to give us the sight of the world bending before the word of our testimony. It was so in apostolic times. Three thousand were converted in one day in one place, and the Lord added to that church daily. A modern writer has observed that in this turning to the Lord on the day of Pentecost, the church was multiplied by twenty-five. That is to say, for every one of those one hundred and twenty disciples God gave twenty-five souls to the church. Such was the effect of the working of the divine power in those first disciples. Holy Ghost power, as the disciple bears testimony to the gospel, passes into and sways the hearer so that he becomes a penitent and a believer. The Christian worker charged with God is a convincing and persuading presence. *If we would see unbelievers under conviction, believers must be filled with the Holy Ghost.* In our work amongst the unsaved, it is only as the power of the Spirit rests upon us, that they will fall like the harvest before the sickle.

The spectacle today is that of a church that can do nothing with and for the world. She tries to think she can. She brags of what she is going to do. She has great and high imaginings of her own importance, and of her proposals, but there is nothing brought to pass of a spiritual order with all her vauntings. The church is powerless. She boasts of a name but is dead while she liveth. She is clever only in the works of the creature, for she is out of touch with God, and what is worse she grieves and resists

The Pentecostal Blessing

the Holy Ghost. There is an unspeakable pathos in this situation. Let us fall prostrate before the Lord, and seek for the church the embodiment of His own ideal for her. He will be found of them who humble themselves. There shall come a lifting up. He will change weakness to strength, fear to courage, barrenness to fruitfulness. The old time power shall return to the church. Sinning men shall be smitten with the distress of conviction, and cry as at the first Pentecost, "Brethren, what shall we do?"

A Holy Ghost church is a growing, increasing, enlarging, multiplying, mighty church. Let us not forget it. There is today a growing, increasing, enlarging, multiplying church, but it lacks the final element—mightiness. The reason of this fatal deficiency is that the Lord is not its Head. The additions of the modern church are mainly of the world and of the flesh. We need to pray against such an increase, but with God the Holy Ghost let there be no fear of multiplication. The Holy Ghost multiplies where He works. He not only fashions the graces of a believer's life, but brings men under the blood of Christ for the remission of their sins. Thousands are converted, multitudes flock to the Lord, and baptisms of the spiritually minded abound. My brethren, let us seek the demonstration of the Holy Ghost. Let us welcome Him in His every manifestation.

O Breath of the Lord blow upon us today, and we shall live in Thy sight, and be what we are called to be, supernatural men among men. O Fire of heaven fall upon us now, and make us a flame in this, our day and generation, that our age may know that Jehovah He is the God, Jehovah He is the God.

Now, in defining Pentecost, we would refer to it as a thing of parts. "The first fruits of the Spirit," a phrase in Rom. 8:23, summarizes those parts. These first fruits are three clusters. We must refer to them under a changed imagery, namely,

The Magnificence of Pentecost

The Sealing. The Earnest. The Anointing.

These three words occur in one passage in 2 Cor. I: "Now He that hath *anointed* us is God, who hath also *sealed* us, and given us the *earnest* of the Spirit in our hearts." The sealing is strikingly referred to as distinct from the first act of faith in verse thirteen of Ist Ephes: "In whom *after that ye believed* ye were sealed with that Holy Spirit of promise." One has but to read the opening verses of the nineteenth of Acts to know how truly distinct was the act of their sealing from the first act of their believing. Then, note the expression: "That Holy Spirit of promise." Wherever you get the word "promise" and "Holy Spirit" in juxtaposition the phrase always refers to the Pentecostal blessing. Now he that is sealed is acquainted with Pentecost in one of its parts. As for the earnest, the light is equally clear connecting it with Pentecostal grace, for in the very next verse to Ephes. I:13 we have such a connection, "That Holy Spirit of promise *which is the earnest.*" As for the *anointing*, it can never be confounded with the new birth. Jesus was born of the Spirit; but it was not until His baptism, when the Holy Ghost descended on Him, that He was anointed. The anointing was for His public ministry. Let us remember that passage in Acts 2:38: "God anointed Jesus of Nazareth with the Holy Ghost and with power, who went about doing good and healing all that were oppressed of the devil." And as He so we. Pentecost in its anointing aspect is for service. But do not let us confine or restrict the meaning of service to Christian work. Not until we are anointed are we free to serve the Lord. We need the anointing for the experience of Christian liberty, as much as for Christian work.

Consider, then, these three parts of the Pentecostal life:

First, the sealing. What is this sealing? It is a property sign. It indicates acknowledgment and ownership. If you are familiar

The Pentecostal Blessing

with life on the western plains you will recall the common scene of the branding of cattle. The initials of the name of a certain man or company are burnt into the animal. That is a seal. So also the stamp which the documents of a public and professional character sometimes contain. The apostle speaks of a personal sealing. He tells us he was branded. "I bear," said he, "in my body the marks of the Lord Jesus." But such sealing is not essentially connected with the Christian life. The sealing of supreme necessity is a spiritual thing entirely. It is what the Scriptures call the *witness* of the Spirit—as in Rom. 8:16, where we read: "The Spirit Himself beareth witness with our spirit that we are the children of God." A Christian writer has aptly referred to the sealing work of the Spirit as the '*upward*' word in the vocabulary of the things of our salvation. It certainly is, for it is the act but which we know ourselves related to the skies. When we are sealed we have no hesitation in believing the two-fold mercy that Christ is ours, and that we are His. The world knoweth us not in this ineffable relationship, but within us is a voice even the voice of the Lord telling us that He acknowledges us as His own. Does the reader know the sealing work of the Spirit of God? If he does he is indeed the blessed of the Lord. My heart goes out in solicitude for such as do not, but if they but hope that they are saved, if they are without the assurance, they are missing the joys of divine life, and possibly may be missing the life itself. *Better a man should never know his own name than not to know the name of Jesus.* If there be doubt and uncertainty we would plead with the reader to make the knowledge of Jesus his supreme business. In doing so he will soon receive the divine attestation of his sonship.

Second, the Earnest. What is the earnest? It is made up of many things. It begins in the sealing for do we not read: "Ye

The Magnificence of Pentecost

were sealed with that Holy Spirit of promise, which is the earnest?" The gospel consists of things to be received, the greatest of which is the inheritance incorruptible, undefiled, unfading, reserved in heaven; the earnest of which, that is to say, the first installment of which are given to us in this life. There is a future salvation, for the Scripture says: "Now is our salvation nearer than when we believed." The salvation in which we now exult, however blessed, is only a small part of our salvation which is treasured up in Christ. Our present salvation is the earnest of the salvation we are to know. Have we now the forgiveness of sins? Are we now the children of God? Presently we are to be delivered from the very presence of sin. Now we are in a sinful world, soon we shall be in a sinless world. Now we are but partially conformed to the divine image, by and by we are to be wholly so. Now as touching sonship we are minors, soon we shall reach that moment which answers in this life to the coming of age in the heir, then we shall have the eternal weight of glory. "The earnest" is a wonderful blessing, for often in speaking of it we have a joy unspeakable and full of glory. But our experiences now are nothing compared with what they will be, for in the ages to come God is going to show—just think of it—the *exceeding riches* of His grace in His kindness towards us through Christ Jesus. What we know now in the earnest is therefore the pledge of coming wonders, blessings magnificent, baffling all description and even conception. As the sealing has been distinguished as the *"upward"* word in the things of our salvation, "the earnest" has been called the *"forward"* word, and rightly so, because he who has it cannot but look forward to what awaits him when he has run his earthly course. Can the reader look ahead and say, "Yonder is my inheritance?" Only such a view is theirs to whom the Lord has vouchsafed in the heart portions of the coming

The Pentecostal Blessing

blessing. May you have the privilege of "the earnest," that you may rejoice in the hope of the glory of God.

Third, the Anointing. As the *sealing* is the sense of relationship, and the *earnest* is the sense of the *eternal inheritance,* the *anointing* is the sense of *enduement.* Many things are involved in the anointing.

First, we may say a pronouncedly spiritual life. This is very clear in Ephesians 5, where the ethical life is seen to depend upon the infilling with the Spirit, for proof of this look at what precedes and follows the Scripture in the eighteenth verse: "Be filled with the Spirit." *This earth witnesses no ethical life according to God's standard of an ethical life apart from souls anointed with the Spirit.* Until a man is filled with the Spirit, he is filled with the self-life, the world is in his heart, and he remains under the partial control of Satan. *The anointing means power,* as it is written: "Ye shall receive power after that the Holy Ghost is come upon you." This is power to speak for Christ, to be witnesses unto Him. The Anointing is also spiritual knowledge, an understanding of our Lord Jesus Christ; for the Spirit searcheth all things, yea, the deep things of God. To them who have received the anointing are the words of John: "Ye have an unction from the Holy One, and ye know all things, and ye need not that any man teach you." There is yet another significance to the word. For the want of a better expression we will call it a *miraculous endowment,* such as is described in I Cor. 12, where the apostle says: "To one is given by the Spirit the word of wisdom; to another the word of knowledge by the same Spirit; to another the working of miracles; to another prophecy; to another discerning of spirits; to another divers kinds of tongues; to another the interpretation of tongues." These are gifts, which, by the way for the most part, are sadly and inexcusably missing from

The Magnificence of Pentecost

the modern church. May they soon be restored, and they will be when the people of God desire God above all things, and serve Him in the passion of true love and holiness.

A like suggestion has been made with reference to the anointing as was made touching the sealing and the earnest. If we regard *the sealing* as the "upward" word, and *the earnest* as the "forward" word in spiritual religion, the anointing must supply us with two more words, so it has been defined as the *"inward"* and the *"outward"* grace. The *"inward"* because of the infilling with the Spirit, the *"outward"* because of the service performed under the power of the enduement and endowment.

Let us here pause to exclaim: "O blessed, blessed, blessed Gift, the Gift of the Holy Ghost!" To know Him in Pentecostal fullness is to know the "upward," the "forward," the "inward" and the "outward" word of the Christian life. Any experience of Pentecost brings at least one of these, but in the fullness of Pentecost the entire four are realized. The *"upward,"* for you then say: "I am Thine and Thou art mine;" the *"forward,"* for you then say: "In my Father's house are many mansions, the glory of which is breaking through and smiting me now;" the "inward," for you then say: "I am filled with the Holy Ghost;" the "outward," for you then say: "I am not ashamed of the gospel of Christ, to me to live is Christ."

> "I'll go where you want me to go, dear Lord,
> Over mountain, o'er plain, o'er sea.
> I'll say what you want me to say, dear Lord;
> I'll be what you want me to be."

By all this the Pentecostal fullness is seen to supply a complete Christian experience. Nothing less, in fact, than a life of

The Pentecostal Blessing

holiness, a life of love, a life of power, and a life of Christ. Such is the glory which the Holy Ghost brings with Him when He comes to us as the Gift. There is no lack. All our desires are quenched and satisfied for we have the very fullness of God.

How beautiful the thought of the possibility of holiness, for holiness is the real Christian's essential character. His calling is a "holy calling." This is the very purpose of God in redemption that we should be "holy and without blame before Him." The new man is "created in righteousness and true holiness." Review the Epistles and see how this thought prevails, I Cor. 3:17. "The temple of God is holy, which temple are ye;" Heb. 3:1. "Holy brethren partakers of the heavenly calling;" I Peter 2:5: "A spiritual house to be an holy priesthood;" Rom. 6:11–13: "Reckon ye yourselves to be dead unto sin, but alive unto God in Christ Jesus. Let not sin therefore reign in your mortal body, that ye should obey the lusts thereof; neither present your members unto sin as instruments of unrighteousness; but present yourselves unto God, as alive from the dead, and your members as instruments of righteousness unto God. For sin shall not have dominion over you." In fact, nowhere will the Word of the Lord permit us to get away from the necessity of holiness for the proper expression of the Christian life. Heb. 12:14: "Follow holiness, without which no man shall see the Lord;" I Peter 1:15: "As He which hath called you is holy, so be ye holy in all manner of living;" Psa. 96:9: "Worship the Lord in the beauty of holiness;" Psa. 93:5: "Holiness becometh Thy house." Such is the testimony. Yet many turn away from it as though it were not Scripture, and as though it were not possible of experience in this life. But how *seriously* the pages of the Word confront us with the possibility and necessity of a holy life here and now, so that he who professes to be the

The Magnificence of Pentecost

Lord's, and does not live a holy life, cannot escape the condemnation of. God. He that is in uncleanness is not a temple of God. "The temple of God is holy." God does not keep company with filth. If we say we have fellowship with Him and walk in darkness, we lie and do not the truth. Pentecost puts within our reach the power of holiness. "God hath chosen you to salvation through sanctification," and the method is "the Spirit and the Word." (II. Thess. 2:14.) The Holy Spirit is given to make the standard a possible and a glorious experience. *The Spirit of Pentecost inaugurates the reign of the law of God in the heart.* The Jews tell us that Pentecost was the time of the year, when the law was announced on Sinai, that Sinaitic law was given fifty days after the original Passover. Such a fact is interesting. The law from Sinai thundered out its demands in the hearing of a helpless people. The anniversary day in the new dispensation, that day of Pentecost, revealed a gift of power, by which all that God is asking of men to do can be done. When you read this Book do you everywhere read of an uncompromising precept? Forget not that gift of Pentecost, the Gift of God Himself, by whom the soul can rise to every duty of the new life. Was the ministry of the law called glorious? Yet was it the ministry of death. "If the ministry of death written and engraved in stone was glorious, so that the children of Israel could not steadfastly behold the face of Moses for the glory of his countenance, how shall not the ministration of the Spirit be rather glorious; for we all with open face beholding as in a mirror the glory of the Lord *are changed into the same image from glory to glory as by the Spirit of the Lord."* Christianity is not natural religion. Let us not say that its ethics for daily life are determined by the possibilities of our nature, for nature never can rise to the knowledge of the Christian life. Christianity is

The Pentecostal Blessing

supernatural religion making possible by the Spirit of the Lord what never can be possible to the flesh. We can escape the lusts of our own nature. We need never be under the bondage of an "I cannot." God stands ready to change "I cannot" to "I can." Sin shall not have dominion over you. The Spirit of the Lord knows of no impossibility. This is the potentiality of Pentecost. People by it are made holy. Sin is taken out of the heart, and even the bias to sin. The heart is made pure, so that you can have your fruit unto holiness, and the end everlasting life. What a glorious gospel! What lustre gathers about the ministration of the Spirit. It puts an end to the life of misery. It deals effectually with the plague of sin. It makes the conquered soul a conqueror. The hitherto defeated soul is led forth in triumph. If you have not so understood the grace of God let your notion of the gospel henceforth be raised. The Lord Jesus Christ never gave us a sinning gospel, that is a gospel that allows sin in the life of them in whom it works. Such a gospel is not the gospel of Christ. A Christian need not consent to sin—the truth must be stated even stronger—the Christian must not consent to sin. He cannot be a Christian if he does. *The Spirit of life in Christ Jesus makes us free from the law of sin and of death.* If you are struggling against sin and beaten in the attempt to overcome, all you need in order to victory, and that an easy victory, is your Pentecost. "Ye shall receive the Gift of the Holy Ghost, for the promise is to all that are afar off." Lift, then, your heart this morning in prayer. Let this be your cry:

"Holy Spirit dwell with me,
I myself would holy be."

But be sure that when you pray you *claim* His indwelling.

The Magnificence of Pentecost

How beautiful the thought of the possibility, of a life of love. Take a look at the early believers. It was their experience. Study the closing passages of Acts 2: "They gladly received His word" (verse 41); "they had all things common" (verse 44); "they did eat their meat with gladness and singleness of heart, praising God" (verses 46, 47). Turn over to Acts 4:32, 33: "And the multitude of them that believed were of one heart, and one soul; neither said any of them that aught of the things which He possessed were His own, but they had all things common." Consider also how much stress the dear Lord laid upon this subject of love. "This is my commandment that ye love one another even as I have loved you." (John 15:12.) "By this shall all men know that ye are my disciples if ye have love one to another." (John 13:35.) And John in his epistle exhorts: "Beloved let us love one another: for love is of God, and everyone that loveth is born of God, and knoweth God. He that loveth not knoweth not God, for God is love." Well then might Paul say: "Though I speak with the tongues of men and of angels and have not love, I am become as sounding brass or a tinkling cymbal. And though I have the gift of prophecy and understand all mysteries and all knowledge: and though I have all faith, so as to remove mountains, and have not love, I am nothing. And though I bestow all my goods to feed the poor, and though I give my body to be burned, and have not love it profiteth me nothing." *Surely we cannot hear such Scriptures as these without realizing how far adrift modern day religion is from the New Testament declaration of Christian life.* As we noted just now, a Christian is a holy being, yet the mass of modern professors ignore this requirement and still account themselves to be of God. How deceived are they. This commandment of love is equally ignored. What is life within the average church? Fault-finding, unkind criticisms,

The Pentecostal Blessing

bitterness, hatred, strife, jealousy, malice, selfishness and covetousness! And the reason is that the churches are without their Pentecost. Pentecost produces the life of love, *love to God*, sympathy with everything of God, so that the work of God, however strange and extraordinary in any human life, in any congregation, is not criticised but an occasion of joy and gratitude. Pentecost produces the life of love, *love to man*. It takes the hardness out of the heart, the harshness out of the tongue, and the unkind look out of the face. A life of love is a life that suffereth long and is kind, that envieth not, that behaveth not itself unseemly, that seeketh not its own, is not easily provoked, and thinketh no evil. Such is the life of love. "The fruit of the Spirit is love, joy, peace, longsuffering, gentleness, goodness, faithfulness, meekness, self-control." The Spirit of God sets everything right within us, and the result is a sweet refreshing life flowing to our neighbor's dwelling, which to him is the water and wine of life. The picture of the renewed soul is like the clear crystal spring. Have you not drawn near and looked to the bottom and watched what is going on with pleasing interest. How the little particles of sand are ever on the move. So it is within the Christian who has had his Pentecost. There is a well of water there, springing up and flowing out. Could you look within, you would see as in the spring, the soul dancing, the heart dancing, the spirit dancing, like those sand particles. Yes, the soul, and heart, and spirit so moving as scarcely to endure the restraints of the body. *The Christian of Pentecost has a life of holy and undying delight.* He is filled with joy and peace in believing, and is abounding in hope through the power of the Holy Ghost. O, he who is flooded with the Spirit is flooded with love, for the love of God is shed abroad in the heart by the Holy Ghost which is given unto us.

The Magnificence of Pentecost

How beautiful the thought also of the possibility of a life of power. This is the most crying of all our needs. How good to feel that a life of power is placed beyond a peradventure in the Word. There, is offered us Pentecost which meets this very need. Necessarily meets it, for Pentecostal life is a life filled with God. He certainly cannot be impotent or feeble who has such a fullness. He cannot be otherwise than a man of strength; strong to be, strong to do, and strong to endure; confronting temptation and overcoming; in suffering unmurmuring, and of exhaustless patience; in duty the soul of faithfulness. The picture will not be that of a ship motionless in the sickly calm of the tropics whose sails flap idly against the masts, and whose pitch oozes from every seam. No, but rather as a vessel in northern waters, a thing of energy and go, ploughing the waters and making for the port at full speed. We have heard Christians sing as if they were doomed to the croaking life:

> "In vain we tune our formal songs,
>   In vain we strive to rise,
> Hosannas languish on our tongues,
>   And our devotion dies."

God never intended such a song for the lips of His people. He never leaves us in the calm of the tropics. He puts us out to sea with a gale at our back, and the gale blows even when we sight the eternal harbor. "Is this dying?" said a saint, who was passing away. The watchers answered, "Yes." "Then," replied he, "I'd just like to go on dying forever." This is the Pentecostal Christian. This is the Pentecostal life. It is a life of power. From the moment we are baptized in the Spirit we are carried away in the will of God. What is His supreme will for us as touching

The Pentecostal Blessing

service? "Ye shall be my witnesses," said He. It is ours to be representing God to man, to be telling the world His truth in Christ Jesus, to be declaring His gospel, to be publishing His name. Is this what Christians as a whole are doing today? Far from it. They professedly accept Christ's salvation, but evidence no constraint to make Him known. Very little perception is there in Christendom of the real nature of the church, for very few comparatively stand for its lofty ideals as proclaimed in the Word. O, for a revival of the conviction that the nature and mission of the church is spiritual. We are to be first, last and all the time missionaries of the cross.

Our great work is to testify of the realities of the things unseen. We are to press home upon the consciences of men the truth of our God. How are professing Christians to get this consciousness? I only know of one way and that by Pentecost: "Ye shall receive power after that the Holy Ghost is come upon you, and ye shall be witnesses unto me," saith Christ. Power and witnessing are conjoined, but the power for witnessing is impossible without the Spirit as the Spirit of Pentecost. *You and I need nothing for the way of the will of God but the Spirit of promise.* The Spirit, remember! Not the hydraulics of human wisdom, not the mechanics of human machinery, but for living Christians, for living churches, for living service the Spirit. *Our only need is the Holy Spirit.* Through the Spirit-filled life of Paul God made the Gentiles obedient by word and deed. "Through mighty signs and wonders by the power of the Holy Ghost." O, for the coming of the Holy Ghost upon the church, then shall we see many a Moses standing before the Pharaohs of the modern world, many an Elijah facing the false prophets of our day, and many a Peter confronting Jerusalem sinners, and many a Stephen telling the truth to a stiff-necked generation; and in

The Magnificence of Pentecost

their mouths "the Word of the Lord will be quick, powerful and sharper than any two-edged sword, piercing even to the dividing asunder of both soul and spirit, and of the joints and marrow, and a discerner of the thoughts and intents of the heart." The world is needing today men of God, not simply men of godly character, but mighty men—John the Baptists, preachers of righteousness, making the age to tremble by reason of its sins.

But such as John the Baptist are not made apart from the Spirit of God. It took the spirit and power of Elias to make a John the Baptist, and that spirit was no less than the Spirit of God. There is nothing equal for the work to be done by the church today but the power of God. A great and conquering future was pointed out by our Lord to His disciples which is a long way from being realized by His present-day followers. "He that believeth on me, the works that I do shall he do also; and, greater works than these shall he do." Words that ought to occasion great heartsearchings everywhere in the church of Christ. O, that the people of God may speedily enquire as to the why and wherefore of their lamentably low estate, and begin to seek their God to the end that they might be the people inheriting the glorious promises intended for fulfillment in the present dispensation.

How beautiful, too, the thought of the possibility in this world of a life of CHRIST. The reflective reader of the New Testament is like the people who were drawn to Christ in the days of His flesh. He is amazed at Christ from every standpoint, whether he considers Him in His character, or speech, or deeds. Every analysis of Christ calls forth his astonishment and he cannot close his study of Him without a sigh and a desire. He will be saying to himself: "I have been reading of a man. The evidence is too great not to regard Him as a man, but He stands out in solitary originality. We have not His like anywhere for goodness, for sympathies, for righteousness, for love, for holiness, and every other attribute of the ideal character. How far away am I from Him. O, that I were like Him." Am I not voicing the sigh and desire of many of you? For your comfort let me remind you that a Christian is predestined to be conformed to His image. But beware of the fatal mistake of not a few who try to be like Christ. You can never be like Him, by absorbing the influences of church-life, not even the purest church life. You cannot get to know Christ by reading books on the imitation of Christ, and books of sacred biography. Christ cannot be incorporated by imitation. Would you be a second edition of Christ, there is only one way, and that, by the infilling with the Holy Ghost. Therefore is it written: "That ye may be strengthened with all might *by His Spirit in the inner man;* that Christ may dwell in your hearts by faith; to the end that ye being rooted and grounded in love may be strong to apprehend with all saints what is the breadth, and length, and height, and depth, and to know the love of Christ which passeth knowledge, that ye might be filled unto all the fullness of God." You see from this that the power of the Spirit of God is the revelation of Jesus Christ in the life. This is a great secret and it is worth knowing. The Spirit of God shall guide you into all truth until you so fully take on Christ that one day you shall awake in His likeness, "A perfect man, the measure of the stature of the fullness of Christ."

CHAPTER 6

The Secrets of Pentecostal Fullness

If the reader has followed us in our thought, he certainly is impressed with the unique conditions involved in being a Christian, and in a congregation being a church. None can be a Christian by a mere say so, and no gathering of people can be a church by resolution, constitution, and an assumption of the name. Spirituality, holiness, love, power, and a life of Christ, however, seem in our day to be no essentials for a Christian life, or that of a church. Rather is this Scriptural conception obsolete, in the minds of professing Christians, and the churches. But this, notwithstanding, we must go on bearing our testimony, that, "Not everyone that saith unto Christ, Lord, Lord, shall enter into the kingdom of heaven, but he that doeth the will of God. The Lord knoweth them that are His: and "Let everyone that nameth the name of the Lord depart from unrighteousness." "In a great house there are not only vessels of gold and of silver, but also of wood and of earth; and some unto honour and some unto dishonour. If a man therefore purge himself from these, he shall be a vessel unto honour, sanctified and meet for the Master's use, prepared unto every good work. But flee youthful lusts, and follow after righteousness, faith, love, peace, with them that call on the Lord out of a pure heart." This is our business. "In meekness correcting them that oppose themselves; if peradventure God may give them repentance unto a knowledge of the truth, and they may recover themselves out of the snare of the devil, having been taken captive by him unto his will." In this concluding chapter on the all-important subject of the Pentecostal Blessing, we come to think of the "how" of the question. The "what" of the question we have seen is the Holy Ghost *as the Gift*. *How are we to know the Holy Ghost in this, His Pentecostal character and fulness?* The answer, on the God side, is simplicity itself, but on the man side an elaborated answer is occasioned by difficulties which there persist, precluding multitudes of desiring souls from ever knowing the Holy Ghost. So I will approach the subject on the man side, and speak of the secrets of or steps to the Pentecostal fulness. They are as follows:

First, cease from sin, in purpose. There must be a readiness of will to have every connection broken between you and sin. This is a stern necessity, before God will give you His best blessing. Look at the adjective that describes and distinguishes the Spirit. He is the *Holy* Spirit. While He finds every man a sinner, His work is to change him into a saint. His work is according to His own character of moral and spiritual perfection. He who would have the Holy Spirit must make up his mind for holiness. The Holy Spirit will not be a companion of him whose life will not bear the light of God's Word, for whatever will not bear the light of that Word is sin, and with sin the Holy Spirit can have no fellowship. Are you, then, ready for a clean sweep of all evil, the least as well as the greatest? Pin your mind down to this issue: "Will I turn from all sin?" "Will I let the Holy Spirit sanctify me?" Do not wander off into sophistical reasoning, and

The Secrets of Pentecostal Fullness

say, as many, "There is no such insistence in the life of the average Christian and church." It is not to their credit that such a thing can be said, and it is one of the reasons, perhaps *the* reason, that they are without the Gift of the Holy Ghost. But YOU wish the Holy Ghost, therefore, you must prepare to be different, to be particular and chasten yourself where they do not. Remember the prevailing religious life is no model for you. A person living the sinning life, providing he does not sin too grossly, may unite with, and stay in, almost any church today, and four-fifths of the Christians of this generation will welcome him to their fellowship, for the obvious reason that they all do the same or similar thing that he is doing. They live the life of pride, vanity, resentment, self-will, anger, malice, back-biting, tale-bearing; are evil-minded, covetous, lustful, respecting the persons of men, lovers of their own way, and rebellious against the ways of the Lord. Do not be deceived by congregations of such, because they bear at the head of their organization the name of Christ. Do not be misled by anyone embodying this evil. A day is coming when God will sweep away every refuge of lies, false churches and Christians not excepted. "Every plant which my heavenly Father hath not planted shall be rooted up."

The only way to assure your heart that you are knowing the blessing of justification is by going on to holiness. None obtain Christian life by church membership, nor by patterning after the ordinary Christian professor. Christian life is only known by the power of the Holy Ghost. Will you have the Holy Ghost? It is useless to desire Him unless your purpose is to cease from sin. Two cannot walk together except they be agreed. We do not say that you must become holy before you can have the Spirit. That were impossible. But you must come to where you

The Pentecostal Blessing

are ready to abandon all sin. It you feel a law working in your members by which you cannot help sinning, will you now say, "I am willing to have the love of sin taken out of me?" If so, you have taken the first step towards a personal Pentecost.

Second, cease from self in purpose. What is Self? It is that thing which is at the back of a life of sin. Scripture knows it as the "carnal mind," "the body of this death." It is the author of the flesh life. If you are afflicted with pride, vanity, resentment, a stubborn will, anger, malice, backbiting, lust and the like, these things are not the source of your trouble. How many after a fit of temper will apologize for the wrong, and in a little while will be as ill-humored as before. Why is this? Because the temper was the expression of a condition. Let the condition be removed and the expression will be lacking. What is the condition which is responsible for all kinds of evil moods and practices? There is but one answer, the presence of Self. Self is a wild beast. When it is quiet we imagine that it has been tamed, that we have it well under control. But suddenly an occasion is precipitated that disturbs our peace. What has happened? The wild beast that is within us has risen and rent us. There can never be any unbroken or appreciable happiness while Self is in the soul, for it is the enemy of all good. In what does real happiness consist, but holiness, a sweet, loving, lovable, beautiful life, Christian peace and joy. Self precludes this experience. It shuts from our life the supernatural. It keeps us in beggary. It cabins, cribs, confines, imprisons and holds in bondage the inner man. It is a tyrant chaining the soul with fear and evil desires, and is death to every noble and blessed impulse and aspiration. The soul that would know Pentecost must be prepared to have Self slain. Will the Holy Spirit come where there is nothing more than a repentance for sin? Nay, there must be a repenting for the Self itself. The cry must be: "O God, deal with the *root* of evil within me. I desire to have done not only with the sinning life but the sinning *nature*, that which *occasions* my trouble, that which holds me a captive, and keeps me a *servant* of sin. Deliver me from Self." Let the reader understand that he cannot be his own deliverer. *There is no such thing as the riddance of Self before the reception of the Holy Ghost.* Only through the Holy Ghost can it be crucified, as it is written: "By the Spirit ye put to death the deeds of the body." The Holy Ghost is our power to drag self from off the throne of the heart and to hang it upon the cross, and to drive such nails through it that it will never come down except for burial. But remember we are not allied to the power of the Holy Ghost until we are willing to surrender Self. The Holy Ghost coming upon the soul constitutes the soul, "the Lord's anointed." Do not confine the anointed ones to the pulpit. The man of the pew who has been filled with the Holy Ghost is as much anointed as the man of God who stands behind the desk. The anointing, however, of any life is impossible where there is no purpose to have Self destroyed. In Exodus 30 we read these words: "Thou shalt anoint Aaron and his son, and sanctify them, that they may minister unto me in the priest's office. And thou shalt speak unto the children of Israel, saying, This shall be a holy anointing oil unto me throughout your generations. *Upon the flesh of man shall it not be poured.*" Here we have a foreshadowing of the truth of this spiritual dispensation. The flesh is a type of Self, and God will neither pour His Holy Spirit upon the flesh life, or upon what occasions it. God will not anoint the nature of sin with His Spirit. Self and the Spirit cannot live together. Therefore, the soul that reaches out for Pentecost, must cease in the purpose of his soul from Self with all its manifestations. Not its manifestations only. He

The Pentecostal Blessing

must go back of pride, vanity, resentment, stubbornness, anger, malice, back-biting, tale-bearing, evil-thinking, covetousness, lust, the respect of the persons of men, the love of having one's own way, and rebellion against God. He must go back of the subtlest expressions, that of making plans for his own life, that of providing entertainment for his own pleasure, that of noting whether men honour him, praise him, look or don't look at him, speak to or slight him. All this ugly sensitiveness is of Self. The branches of this evil tree must be cut down, but more, the axe must be laid at its very root. We must get to where the expressions are non-existent and that we never do until Self is *crucified*. If Self is on the throne of your being with your own consent, vain will be your expectation of the Spirit of God. As long as you permit Self to fill you, God will wait until you are sick of Self before He will do His great work in you, for know this, God is not asking for a mere surface to cover but a vacuum to fill. Clear the way, then, for your personal Pentecost by taking these two preparatory steps. Be it yours to say: "By the grace of God, I will have done with sin, I will have done with Self."

Now there are certain tests by which one may know whether he has taken these two steps. Let me suggest what they are. *Will I accept every manifestation of the Spirit of God in others? Will I receive whatever the Spirit of God determines as my life work? Will I obey unquestioningly and instantly the leadings of the Spirit? Will I be still before God? Will I believe God? Will I glorify Christ?* If each of these is punctuated by the "Amen" of the heart, all that remains for the knowledge of the Spirit in Pentecostal fullness is prayer.

If Pentecost is to be an experience the Christian must remember the object of redemption. When man sinned, the government of human life shifted to man himself. Man took the reins out of God's hands, and that act made him a sinner. Man's life has never been right since that day. In order to creature rectitude man must restore to God what he stole from God. Provision has been made for this in the gospel. One of the most luminous passages of Scripture bearing upon this truth is found in Psa. 69:4, where the Saviour says: *"I restored that which I took not away."* Significant words. Ponder them. Jesus did not wrest the sceptre of man's life from the hands of God. That was our act. But Jesus stepped into our place when He suffered on the cross, and not only paid the penalty for our transgressions, but by His precious, wounded, pierced, bleeding Hands, He took the sceptre of God's sovereignty over the creature, out of the hands of the creature, and placed it back into the hands of God. Yes, said He, "I restored that which I took not away." So, then, it follows that every one who is summed up in Jesus Christ not only has escaped the leash of the law, but is put back under the sovereignty of God. This is not what the mass of professing Christians have understood by the cross of Christ. The work of the gospel is not only the forgiveness of sins, eternal life, and sonship for the creature, *but God's unrestrained lordship over body, soul and spirit;* over all, all that we are, all that we have, all that we shall be, and all that we shall have. Are you prepared for this? It involves, as we have said, first,

The acceptance of every manifestation of the Spirit of God in others.

He who is prepared for this ceases to criticize other people in their spiritual exercises. When God works He asks no man what form of manifestation of Himself will suit him in his community life. Whether He shall come as a still small voice or as a tempest; whether as an earthquake or silently as the rising sun; whether as a burning, blazing fire, or as the moistening

The Pentecostal Blessing

dew; whether as the rushing mighty wind breaking the cedars of Lebanon, or as a gentle, zephyr not breaking the bruised reed nor quenching the smoking flax; whether as a driving or drawing power; whether in threatenings or in promises; whether to make this and that man Boanerges, or as Barnabas. God is sovereign. So few have learned this truth, therefore are there but few who have received the Holy Ghost. A revival is God at work, and no one can tell how God is going to work. We must be prepared for anything he desires to do. We of ourselves are not able to bless this world. Man is a total failure at the work of bringing heaven on earth. Let him then step aside and let God do what he cannot do, and let God do it in His own way. He that will not consent to this will grieve the Holy Spirit and forfeit his Pentecost. When the Holy Spirit comes with convicting grace, souls frequently cry out in their distress. If we desire to be people after the Lord's own heart, we must not resent the deep work of the Spirit in our fellow creatures. At such times what you hear is just the sound of God's quarry blasting which must take place before the stone can be separated, and fitted into the temple of the Lord. When you hear the shout of some saint hesitate to take an exception, for it may be the very shout of God. There is a Scripture that says: "Cry out and shout, thou inhabitant of Zion, for great is the Holy One of Israel in the midst of thee." There will be something heard in the earth when it can be said of the Lord's people that the shout of the King is among them. It is not the nature of life to be silent as the grave. Where there is an increase of life there is likely to be an increase of expression. If you see a jumping saint, do not take offense and readily conclude fanaticism. God's quarried blocks, according to Peter are *lively* stones. If you will let the thrilling truths of the gospel work in you, a wonder will seize you, not that anyone should leap for joy, but that anyone should be quiet, sedate, passionless. "With joy shall ye draw water out of the wells of salvation." News comes to us of a revival in India, where there are extraordinary manifestations of the Spirit of God. A correspondent tells us that in singing, the converts wave their hands and jump and dance. They cannot restrain themselves in hymns expressing the love of God and their triumph over Satan. Is the Spirit of the Lord straitened? Nay, and you may as well try to seal the wind, and still the pulsing of the tides as to silence the Holy Ghost. He is a free Spirit. He shines as the sun. He leaps, like a roe or a young hart upon the mountains of spices. Would we know Him, we must cease our prejudices and stand for the right of the Spirit of God to speak as He will, by whom He will, and when He will. If anything that the Spirit of God is, or does, grates on our feelings, the grating, remember, is on the feelings of Self. Self never approves of God, and will take sides against God. The spiritual is an offense to it. Therefore must Self be put away. Have you put it away? You may test yourself by this sign. Will I accept every manifestation of the Spirit of God in others? Next,

Will I receive whatever the Spirit of God determines as my life work and obey unquestioningly and instantly the leadings of the Holy Ghost?

Very often in talking to the seeker of the Spirit-filled life it is necessary to call attention to the *consequences* of the Spirit's in-coming, the all-round consequences. He who wakes up to find that the full meaning of redemption is the sovereignty of God over the individual frequently finds an unlooked-for future opening up to him. Sometimes the Spirit's infilling results in

The Pentecostal Blessing

the consequence of what the world would call the lowliest service. Are you willing to go into obscurity and never have your deeds trumpeted to the world or even spoken of in the church? Sometimes the infilling calls for great sacrifices—the sacrifice of money, home, companionship, friends, and every earthly delight. Are you prepared for this. He who would have the Holy Ghost must think more of God than of anything or anyone else. Will you count it a joy to relinquish all for the Lord. He may not require it but if He does will you say yes to Him. To say yes to God is to be on the eve of a splendid mercy from God. For saith He: "There is no man that hath left house, or brethren, or sisters, or father, or mother, or wife, or children, or lands, for my sake and the gospel's, but he shall receive a hundred-fold *now in this time*, houses and brethren, and sisters, and mothers, and children, and lands, with persecutions; and in the world to come eternal life." Say, then, unto your soul, "Rise up, O, my soul, and follow the Lamb whithersoever He leadeth. Over mountains and through valleys, arctic regions or tropics, civilization or the habitations of cruelty, thick thoroughfares or desert wastes, flames, floods or blood, where He leads me I will follow, and go with Him all the way."

Again, *the stillness of the soul before God is a factor in the knowledge of the Spirit.* So few in the household of God ever seem to know a quiet time before God. There is either a rush in the soul or a rush in the life, and sometimes both. Now God wants a hush where there's a rush. It is specially desirable that those seeking the Holy Spirit should realize this. Take time to be holy. Be still. If you are without your Pentecost you had better cease your work. Is this a startling proposition? Are you thinking of how much there is to do, and of the millions of souls that are dying. Remember, there was much to do in the days of the risen Christ, and souls were dying then as they do now, but He said to His disciples, "Wait, tarry until ye be endued with power from on high." Dear reader, you can do more in five minutes with the power of the Holy Ghost than you can do in fifty years without that power. The years of the silent life of Jesus were thirty, and His active years but three. He waited for His baptism of power. The servant is not greater than His Lord. The first disciples waited for ten days. It is not now necessary to wait for God to move. He has moved and is moving. He has given the Spirit from heaven. The Spirit is not an absent Lord but right with the reader. If you have not been filled with Him, if you are without the enduement with power be silent before God. We mean now not prayer, but a real silence. Cease anxiety. Be not feverish. Be quiet and listen to God. He wishes to say something to you. Let Him speak. It may be that He wants to go over your life. It may be that He wants to occupy you with His Word. Whatever it may be, listen. Be taken up with Him. One in a certain place, who had passed through this experience testified of the result in the following verse. What if you should need such a time before the Lord?

> "My hands were filled with many things
>   That I did precious hold,
> As any treasures of a king's—
>   Silver, or gems, or gold.
> The Master came and touched my hands,
>   (The scars were in His own)
> And at His feet my treasures sweet
>   Fell shattered, one by one.
> 'I must have empty hands,' said He,
>   'Wherewith to work My works through thee.'

The Pentecostal Blessing

"My hands were stained with marks of toil,
   Defiled with dust of earth;
And I my work did oft times soil,
   And render little worth.
The Master came and touched my hands,
   (And crimson were His own)
But when amazed, on mine I gazed,
   Lo! every stain was gone.
'I must have cleans'd hands,' said He,
'Wherewith to work My works through thee.'

"My hands were growing feverish,
   And cumbered much with care.
Trembling with haste and eagerness,
   Nor folded oft in prayer.
The Master came and touched my hands,
   (With healing in His own)
And calm and still to do His will,
   They grew—the fever gone.
'I must have cleansed hands,' said He,
'Wherewith to work My works through thee.'

"My hands were strong in fancied strength,
   But not in power divine,
And bold to take up tasks at length,
   That were not His, but mine.
The Master came and touched my hands,
   (And might was in His own)
But mine since then have powerless been,
   Save His are laid thereon.
'And it is only thus,' said He,
'That I can work My works through thee.'"

O, is it not worth while to be quiet before the Lord, to let Him search us, to let Him discover to us ourselves? *You see it all ends in our discovery of Him.* As soon as He has an opportunity to prepare us, He pervades us, and we rise to go forth strong in the might of His power.

Quietness before the Lord will lead to prayer.

God will draw out the soul in petition. He will say: "What wilt thou that I should give thee. Take with you words." For our responses to Him He has abundantly provided. Consider the exceeding great and precious promises. Shall we not call them *The Prayer Permits* of the Word? "Ask, and it shall be given you; seek, and ye shall find; knock, and the door shall be opened unto you; for every one that asketh receiveth; and he that seeketh findeth; and to him that knocketh the door shall be opened." "If ye, then, being evil, know how to give good gifts unto your children: how much more shall your heavenly Father give the Holy Spirit to them that ask him?" These, and many other Scriptures will be the prevailing notes of our intercession. *In prayer for the Spirit, the soul will plead the fact of an ascended Christ.* Our Lord said to His first disciples: "Ye shall be baptized in the Holy Ghost not many days hence." After He was taken up from them, and they were in prayer in that upper room, may we not conclude that this was one of the arguments they used in waiting for the promise of the Father? Thou didst say: "It is expedient for you that I go away; for if I go not away, the Comforter will not come unto you; but if I depart I will send Him unto you." Did not they also think of Psa. 68: "Thou hast ascended on high, thou hast led captivity captive; thou hast received gifts for men; yea, for the rebellious also, that the Lord God might dwell among them?" Enriched with the promises, they must have pleaded them. Heaven must have heard

The Pentecostal Blessing

the argument of Gethsemane and Calvary; the argument of the passion, the bloody sweat, and sacrificial death; the argument of the resurrection and the session at the right hand of God. And so will heaven be hearing these arguments by those who today seek their Pentecost: "Lord, are not all things ready? Am not I? Didst Thou not proclaim upon the cross a finished work?"

> "Jesus thou art gone up on high:
> But Thy promise still is here;
> I will all your wants supply,
> I will send the Comforter."

> "Send me, Lord, the Comforter,
> Pledge and witness of Thy love."

Following upon prayer, nay, rather in prayer, there must be faith. *A believing of God*. Not all who recognize the truth of the Gift of the Spirit, and who ask for the Spirit, receive Him, because there is no boldness of faith, no confidence of assurance in their petition. See to it, dear reader, that you have a full persuasion that the Lord *will* bless *you*. Without this conviction you will fail to get anywhere in relation to the blessing. It must be a settled confidence within you that our wonder-working God will indwell you in fullness. There is such a thing for every child of God as the communion of the Holy Ghost. Jesus said: "I will send *you* another Comforter." "The promise is to *all* who *are* afar off." Do you regard yourself as one afar off? Well blessed be God the afar off ones are included, and of these the weak, the ignorant, the insignificant, the infinitesimal units! Do not have your eye on Moses and Elijah and the like, and tremble to hope. They were men of like passions

The Secrets of Pentecostal Fullness

as ourselves. Bear in mind that all that ever makes any man great is the blessing of the Lord. The Lord God stands ready this very moment to make your little life great, and give power to a worm to thrash a mountain. If you will believe you shall be endued with power from on high. The promised blessing is wonderful, but let no one draw back because of the amazing glory of it. "Ask and ye shall receive." Ask for the Spirit and God will give you no less. He has pledged to give this. He binds Himself to so bless the believer. What great encouragement, then, you can have in seeking the Spirit. When upon the oath of His word the Spirit is promised, wonder not that if you draw back from believing you cannot be established. Until faith springs up within you it is impossible for God to bless you. The mercy tarries until you believe. When we believe for the Holy Ghost the Holy Ghost comes. Do you press the question: "How am I to receive the Spirit?" "Faith" is the answer, for it is written: "Christ hath redeemed us from the curse of the law . . . that we might receive the promise of the Spirit *through faith*." (Gal. 3:13, 14.) "But what if I do not feel?" perhaps you are saying, "has the Spirit come to me?" Yes, if you are believing. These thoughts of your mind are suggestive. We are reminded by them of those who can look back upon a definite reception of the Holy Ghost, but who today know not a life inspired in all the will of God. Lest after receiving the Spirit you should fall into their error, we tarry to account for their condition. At the time of their baptism in the Holy Spirit they put forth an act of faith and received accordingly, then they rested in the sufficiency of that act which brought the Holy Ghost and failed in a *continuous* exercise of their faith. The Spirit, like the Saviour only responds to faith. There is no "once for all" experience in the reception of the Holy Ghost. The truth relative

The Pentecostal Blessing

to this has been stated so admirably by that prince of preachers, Dr. Maclaren, that we will quote his words: "The Spirit of God," says he, "and the power which comes from Him, are not given as a purse of money might be put into a man's hand once and for all, but they are given in a continuous impartation and communication, and are received and retained moment by moment, according to the energy of our desires, and the faithfulness of our use." Only then is the fullness yours as moment by moment you believe. After your baptism in the Spirit keep your faith a-going and your Pentecost will be perpetual. The Christian life is a life of faith. There is no other way by which a Christian can live. The Holy Spirit, as was the Saviour, is taken by faith. When taken by faith He is with you as surely as when you believed on Jesus you received the Saviour. It did not depend on feeling whether Jesus had come in, neither is feeling a condition for the reception of the Holy Ghost. To believe is to receive. If you have really believed for the Holy Ghost you have received Him, feeling or no feeling. Be like the little child when you have no feeling on a spiritual subject. She was asked her age, and she made reply: "I don't feel like seven, I feel like six, but Mother says I am seven." The little child rested on what her mother said and you must rest on what God says. "If ye then being evil know how to give good gifts unto your children, *how much more* shall your heavenly Father give the Holy Spirit to them that ask Him." Live standing on the promises of God. God may test your faith. Will you not let Him do so if He so desires? He may not give you for awhile a sweet sense of the glory of His indwelling, but forget not that when you believe He honors your faith by the Gift to you of the Holy Ghost. It is faith that brings the Spirit, and God will not leave you long without the witness of His glorious presence,

The Secrets of Pentecostal Fullness

and such a witness it will be that heaven and earth and hell will know that you are filled with the Spirit of the living God.

With every experience of Pentecostal fulness there is a demonstration. It may not be as the rushing mighty wind, or as tongues of fire. But there will come with it many changes. Let us think of a few of them.

A sense of the sacredness of your being. The truth that you are a temple of the Holy Ghost will profoundly enter into your consciousness, and you will keep yourself unspotted from the world. Tastes, ambitions, likes and loves will all be of a different order and in keeping with the dwelling place of God.

You will have clean escaped from the hold of Satan.

Whatever he may do, whatever be his traps and tricks, however subtle his strategy, he will not be able to entice you from your integrity and devotion to God. Your victory will be easy over the world, the flesh and the devil.

You will delight in the prayer life.

We shall hear you saying and singing: "There is nothing like communion with my Saviour." He will be very real and precious to you.

Circumstances will have no power to annoy.

If you are treated badly, cheated, wronged, regarded unkindly, spoken against falsely, and the keen winds of adversity blow your way, none of these things will be a worry. Pentecostal Christians have rest in every trial, for they know their times are in God's hands, and there is no evil that can befall them. They remember the Scriptures: "Who is he that can harm you if ye be followers of that which is good?" "No good thing will He withhold from them that walk uprightly." "All things work together for good to them that love God." No circumstance can disturb their quiet and assurance, their peace and joy. Their life

The Pentecostal Blessing

as a result is as a poured forth alabaster box of fragrant spikenard, and the privilege is great to live where they live. *Abounding blessings enrich both soul and body knowing the power of the Spirit.*

The glory of His presence causes our physical being to take on new life. That word is true. "If the Spirit of Him that raised up Jesus from the dead dwell in you. He that raised up Christ from the dead shall also quicken your mortal bodies by His Spirit that dwelleth in you." And who shall tell of its wonders over the soul. Let the changes Peter knew in his Pentecost suffice to illustrate our thought. We may know them all in believing: For, he that believeth on me, as the Scripture hath said, out of his belly shall flow rivers of living water. This spake He of the Spirit that they which believe on Him should receive." The Spirit of God yields Himself to the trusting heart, and the effect is the overflowing life. Faith clears the channel for the incoming of the Spirit, and having entered, He fills us, and from out of us go forth divine influences and inspirations as from a center, and the church and the world become effectually blessed in our presence.

Once more and we have done. *Be ready to glorify our Lord Jesus Christ.* Have you attended to this? It is by no means the least item in the preparation for Pentecost. John 7:38, 39 is not to be regarded as of historical import only. The words are a suggestion. "The Holy Ghost was not yet given because Jesus was not yet glorified." The passage refers to the ascension, but we may gather another meaning. *Some are without their Pentecost because they have not exalted the Lord Jesus Christ.* The Holy Spirit is not yet given, because Jesus is not yet glorified. For what do you desire the baptism in the Spirit? That you might be something? That is an unworthy motive. The Holy Spirit is never given for the manifestation of us but the manifestation of Christ. Do you want Him that you may be able to do something? Where He comes it is to do something through the individual, not that the individual should do something, or that he might be some great one. God does not come to help us out in any of our schemes. We cannot command Him if we wish to use Him. The Holy Spirit is given solely to magnify Christ in us, and through us. We, like John the Baptist, decrease, and He increases.

Ours is a high destiny in being the dwelling place of our God. How the thought should humble us, and how ready we ought to be to shrink to nothingness, that He may be all in all. What a fellowship, Christ in us, the Christ of the throne, the Christ of the incarnation, the Christ of the cross, the Christ of the resurrection, the Christ of the atonement, the Christ who has vanquished death and hell, the Christ who has brought life and incorruptibility to light through the Gospel. Of this Christ may we say, "Let Him be glorified." Let the redeemed of the Lord say so, whom He has delivered from the hand of awful enemies. Can we do less with Him than nations do with their heroes? Think of Rome. How the Senate decreed for victorious generals the worship of a god. Think of what happened, for instance, upon the return of Paulus Aemilius to Rome, having triumphed over Macedonia, holding captive Perseus, its defeated king. The conqueror was placed in a chariot hitched to milk-white steeds and drawn through the streets to the Capitol amid the plaudits of the world. For the day he was the greatest man in all the earth, greater than the emperor. What a sight, that triumphal car. How impressive the victory, as those prisoners of war were seen chained at the feet of the hero. What a day for Rome. The multitude gave its praise and the general in return showered upon the heads of the vast concourse the coin of the realm. This is how men act towards an earthly hero, and an earthly hero acts towards his admirers. What may we not expect of Jesus if only we will crown Him Lord of all. Crown Him, brother. Crown Him, sister. Crowns become the victor's brow. The Holy Spirit has not been bestowed in the blessed way God would give Him, because Jesus has not yet been glorified among His people. "Who is this that cometh from Edom with dyed garments from Bozrah, this that is glorious in His apparel, traveling in the greatness of His strength?" Lo! 'tis Jesus, the greatest of the conquerors. He hath vanquished all the enemies of God and man, and chained to His chariot the chief of rebels. Behold Him in His triumphal car. He leads captivity captive. He has gifts for men. Salvation, and the Promise of the Father—the Holy Spirit. Salute Him. Glorify Him. Cry aloud, "All hail the power of Jesus' name," and ye shall receive the Gift of the Holy Ghost.

> "Crown Him with many crowns,
>   The Lamb upon His throne:
> Hark! how the heavenly anthem drowns
>   All music but its own.
> Awake! my soul, and sing
>   Of Him who died for thee;
> And hail Him as thy matchless King,
>   Through all eternity."

Biographies of Azusa Street Book Series Editors

Cecil M. Robeck Jr., PhD, is an ordained Assemblies of God minister who has served on the administration and faculty of Fuller Theological Seminary for over forty years. He is currently senior professor of Church History and Ecumenics and special assistant to the president for Ecumenical Relations. He has two academic passions. The first is the Azusa Street Mission and the revival that exploded there in April 1906. The second is working with Christian leaders all over the world on issues related to the unity of Christ's Church.

Darrin Rodgers, M.A., JD, is director of the Flower Pentecostal Heritage Center (Springfield, Missouri), the Pentecostal archives and research center located in the National Leadership and Resource Center of the Assemblies of God. He also serves as editor of *Assemblies of God Heritage* magazine.

Author of "Joseph Smale: A Biographical Sketch"

Tim Welch, PhD, is tutor and coordinator of Ministerial Formation at Bristol Baptist College (Clifton Down, Bristol, United Kingdom). Like Joseph Smale, he trained for Baptist ministry at Spurgeon's College in London.